MW00818128

Six Shifts to Improve Special Education and Other Interventions

Six Shifts to Improve Special Education and Other Interventions

A COMMONSENSE APPROACH FOR SCHOOL LEADERS

NATHAN LEVENSON

Harvard Education Press

Cambridge, Massachusetts

Paperback ISBN 978-1-68253-479-3
Library Edition ISBN 978-1-68253-480-9

Library of Congress Cataloging-in-Publication Data
Names: Levenson, Nathan, author.
Title: Six shifts to improve special education and other interventions : a commonsense approach for school leaders / Nathan Levenson.
Description: First. | Cambridge, Massachusetts : Harvard Education Press, [2020] | Includes index. | Summary: "Six Shifts to Improve Special Education and Other Interventions offers a set of bold, new ideas for dramatically raising the achievement of students with mild to moderate disabilities and students experiencing serious academic, social and emotional, and behavioral difficulties"— Provided by publisher.
Identifiers: LCCN 2019060166 | ISBN 9781682534793 (paperback) | ISBN 9781682534809 (library binding)
Subjects: LCSH: Special education—United States. | Students with disabilities— United States—Services for. | Learning disabled children—Education. | Developmentally disabled children—Education. | Inclusive education—United States. | School management and organization—United States. | Special education teachers—United States.
Classification: LCC LC4704 .L49 2020 | DDC 371.9—dc23
LC record available at https://lccn.loc.gov/2019060166

Published by Harvard Education Press,
an imprint of the Harvard Education Publishing Group

Harvard Education Press
8 Story Street
Cambridge, MA 02138

Cover Design: Wilcox Design
Cover Image: Chris Ryan/OJO Images via Getty Images

The typefaces used in this book are Sabon and Milo OT

This book is for all the dedicated staff and leaders who have worked so hard to help kids who struggle, for the parents who have worked tirelessly to navigate a too-complex system in order to ensure their children's needs are met, and for the visionaries who realize that we owe them something better and different, not just a bit more of past practices.

More than half the students in our schools struggle academically, have social and emotional needs that are unmet, and leave twelfth grade not fully prepared for success in a complex world. I hope this book shows a practical path to improve the lives of these struggling children. This book is for everyone who wants to help them.

CONTENTS

CHAPTER 1

A Personal Journey to a Better Place

I'M NOT SURE what's more surprising: that forty-five years after the passage of the Education for All Handicapped Children Act of 1975, the predecessor of the Individuals with Disabilities Education Act (IDEA), I'm suggesting that the long-held common wisdom about how best to serve struggling students with and without special needs ought to change, or so few others are demanding a change. Perhaps in the same way that fish don't see or feel water (so I'm told), most educators and parents alike have come to accept the current approach to special education and response to intervention (RTI) and multitiered system of supports (MTSS) as part of the bricks and mortar of our schools.

During my fifty-year journey, I've come to believe that special education, RTI/MTSS, and other supports for struggling students need a commonsense redesign to meet the needs of students in the twenty-first century. The world has changed, and so must schools' support of students with disabilities and others who struggle.

I have experienced firsthand the need for IDEA and its assurance of help, but also its shortcomings. Fortunately, I have also seen the path to much higher achievement, even in times of tight resources.

Even before I entered kindergarten, I needed special education services, but when I was born in 1961, schools weren't then required to help me. It took nine years until such services became a right. My mother, a woman who took every challenge seriously, dedicated endless hours and significant expense to address a serious speech impediment. She drove me an hour each way, twice a week, for services. She also battled mightily with teachers who couldn't understand why I sometimes missed school to make these appointments.

As my speech improved, my dysgraphia become more problematic. My handwriting was unreadable and my spelling horrific, but my comprehension, analysis, and thought processes were not too bad. Again, my mom battled the school's perception that I was too lazy to write and spell well and that my well-reasoned but poorly scribed English papers shouldn't get an F, even if my spelling was problematic. Without a few tense meetings with the principal and much perseverance by my mother, I would have been denied access to accelerated math and advanced reading due to my poor spelling and handwriting.

Today, thanks to my mother and despite my school, I regularly speak nationally to large audiences and have written a number of books and dozens of articles. As a student, I was disappointed that my schools couldn't or wouldn't help me and that kids like me who needed something more and different didn't seem to fit into the systems and structures available.

Years later, as an adult, I reconnected with the realities of special education on my first day as a school board member. While running for the seat, I had heard from taxpayers that special education costs were rising fast, and I learned from teachers that special education was "complicated," but nothing had prepared me for my first board meeting.

The special education director had requested time on the agenda. At around 10:30 p.m., tired and wanting to go home, the director finally got his chance to address the school board. He seemed more tired than me. Calmly he said that he was resigning because the district wasn't serving its struggling students well and he didn't know how to fix it but couldn't continue to be part of a broken system any longer. This said, he sat up straight, gained some vigor, and enumerated a number of issues:

- We wait for kids to fail before we offer help.
- When we do help, few students ever catch up to their nonstruggling peers.

- Too many hard-working, caring staff are stressed, exhausted, and burning out due to seemingly endless paperwork and meetings.
- While we embrace inclusion, too many general education teachers are hoping that special education will solve most every social, emotional, behavioral, and academic need of our students.

And on he went. He felt guilty when he asked for more staff each year, and even guiltier that he couldn't provide all the supports our kids needed and most guilty that he didn't know what to do differently to move the needle on achievement.

Shell-shocked at both his candor and the troubling picture he painted, I listened and took copious notes, my handwriting still hard to read. What happened next was, perhaps, more surprising. The superintendent and principals assured the board and the community not to worry. Special education is hard, and every district is striving to improve. They didn't say the complaints were unjustified, just commonplace. We struggled to meet the needs of struggling students, and so did most other districts. That was their message.

Over the next five years, both formally and informally, I researched how schools served struggling students, with and without special needs. I met lots of administrators who shared the feeling that something ought to change, but mostly that entailed just a bit more of the same. A few more special education teachers, a couple of paraprofessionals, or another speech therapist. The staff I met wanted relief from the paperwork and meetings, but generally were satisfied with what they did when they had direct time with students. The staff also wanted smaller caseloads to make the work more manageable. Parents wanted much better outcomes for their children, but again this usually meant more (a lot more) of the same.

After crisscrossing the country, interviewing hundreds of frontline educators and school and district administrators, I found that nearly everyone wanted something better. They wanted to tweak the system, but most accepted the current approach as worthwhile and fundamentally sound. This surprised me for three reasons:

1. Student achievement was chronically low.
2. Too few college grads wanted to become (or stay) a special educator.
3. Spending kept rising, but outcomes didn't.

As a school board member, I was unhappy with the status quo, but like so many others I had met along this journey, I didn't know how to make things better. Fortunately, I had also discovered along the way some forward-thinking, innovative teachers, principals, and administrators who saw a better approach for helping kids who struggled.

As a child, I had looked up and seen, felt, and struggled with the supports provided to a student who needed more to achieve at high levels. As an adult, I have looked around for a better way to help kids in need.

After nearly twenty years of study, research, and hands-on experience in schools, I have seen what's needed to update special education and other interventions for the new era. Something needs to change, for the sake of the kids. In fact, six shifts have to take place:

1. *From special education to general education.* While special education shouldn't fade away, general education and core instruction must play a bigger role.
2. *From more adults to more time.* Adding more adults hasn't helped enough but giving students more time to master grade-level content has.
3. *From generalists to specialists.* Struggling students need the most effective teachers in the school with deep content knowledge, subject-specific training, and a track record of high student growth. Asking special educators to be Jacks and Jills of one thousand trades isn't fair to them or their students.
4. *From deterrence to prevention.* Meeting the social, emotional, and behavioral needs of students is a prerequisite to addressing their academic needs and addressing the root cause of

problematic behaviors. It creates an atmosphere where teachers can teach and students can learn.

5. *From one good schedule to many great schedules.* Without a systems-thinking, districtwide approach to scheduling, these best practices get watered down, undermined, or just not delivered with available staffing levels. Great schedules make them possible.

6. *From managing compliance to managing practice, too.* As services and teacher practice change, so must the roles of leaders and managers. Compliance can't drop, but effective implementation must become the top priority.

These ideas may, at first, seem counterintuitive. Less special education for kids who struggle. Fewer suspensions for kids who act out. More management, a new organizational chart, and a fixation with scheduling. Yup, it's different, but I didn't arrive at it hastily.

This approach is based on best practices I identified in published research combined with in-depth research that I and my firm, the District Management Group, have undertaken in 125 school districts over the past ten years. This research has included focus groups with more than five thousand educators, reviews of schedules from nearly fifty thousand special education or general education interventionists, school psychologists, social workers, and counselors, and studies of "achievement-gap-closing" schools and districts that have been effective in improving the outcomes of struggling students.

Beyond extensive research of what works, I have also helped more than a hundred districts actually implement these ideas. The districts cover more than half the United States and range in size from fewer than a hundred students to more than a million and everything in between. They serve rich and poor in equal measure and also include some charter schools. My implementation experience provided practical insights, lessons learned, and pitfalls to avoid.

The ideas are getting traction and have been incorporated in administrator preparation or development programs in Florida, Louisiana, Connecticut, Massachusetts, Vermont, and elsewhere. Most importantly, the shifts have created meaningful improvement in real-life districts. Proof of success includes:

- One district had more *students with disabilities* score proficient or better on the state assessments than the statewide average for *general education* students. Overall, it had the highest achievement of students with disabilities in the state and fully embraced the six shifts.
- One district reduced the special education–general education achievement gap in both math and English by approximately forty points at the high school level over three years.
- One district increased the number of students with disabilities making more than a year's gain by 20 percent in both math and English over two years, districtwide.
- A large, urban school reduced major behavioral incidents from 341 to 66 over four years.
- One district reduced by half the number of students needing special education services in its elementary schools over three years, to the delight of parents and teachers.
- One district saw all twenty-four elementary schools improve in reading with as many as 21 percent more students reading at grade level.
- One district tripled the number struggling freshmen reaching grade level in math, from 21 percent at grade level to 67 percent over two years.
- One district increased counseling services threefold without adding new staff or spending.
- One district added daily intervention blocks in twenty-one schools without adding staff, lengthening the school day, or reducing time for music, art, or PE.

I hope these success stories will motivate you to learn, get angry, and take action. This book will guide school and district leaders, both within and outside special education, with a few new ideas and a whole lot of practical advice on how to turn concepts into reality within the complex, political world that is preK–12. I hope policy makers, thought leaders, influential parents, and others will also read this book, see the world differently, and support the needed shifts in our schools.

The book comprises three parts. In this chapter, I will try to get you riled up. The world has changed, and so must how we serve kids in need. Chapters 2 through 8 cover each of the six shifts from concept to practice to lessons learned. Shift #4, addressing social emotional and behavioral supports, is so important that it gets two chapters. Finally, I end with a few thoughts on how to build a coalition to lead the effort demanding a new approach to help kids in need.

WHY CHANGE?

If you are ready to roll up your sleeves and work to change how struggling students are served in preK–12, if you believe with your heart and soul they deserve better, and if you are certain that just tweaking the current system won't vault these kids into success after graduation, then you can skip the rest of this section. If, however, you are thinking some things could be better, but let's not throw out the baby with the bath water or if you are holding out for a bit more staffing and better professional development, then read on. Our approach to serving students who struggling with and without special needs must change.

Since the early days of No Child Left Behind, the country learned a dirty little secret. Even in the highest-performing schools in all fifty states, kids with disabilities seldom mastered grade-level material or graduated from college. Equally alarming, far too many students without disabilities also struggled mightily and seldom caught up. In the decades since the first statewide tests, US schools have upped their game in K–12 for many children, but not all. More students are proficient, will graduate, and will enter the middle class, but unfortunately the gap between kids living in poverty or with disabilities has widened. A rising tide didn't raise all boats. We are still leaving too many children behind. To add insult to injury, these students are disproportionately students of color. The drive to improve equity and the effort to better serve struggling students are deeply interconnected.

Fourth-grade reading scores have barely budged despite massive efforts focusing on early literacy, RTI, MTSS, and significant increases in special education spending. From 2002 to 2017, scores rose just three points on a five-hundred-point scale.[1] The average student in the United States scored eighteen points below proficient in 2017. By this measure, more than half the kids in the country are struggling students. Worse yet, all of this meager gain came from higher-performing students doing a bit better. Kids at the bottom aren't improving. In 2017, National Assessment of Education Progress (NAEP) achievement actually declined for students with disabilities. The 2017 results match those of 2003.

One award-winning district exemplifies current reality. A large, thirty-thousand-plus student district, under a strong, visionary leader, it changed the course of the lives of many of its students. After it laid the groundwork, great things happened. Students in every grade, in every subject, had achieved more growth than in every other district in the state. Then they repeated this best-in-state accomplishment two more years in a row. Amazing and inspiring, but only sort of. During this same period of rapid growth in student achievement, a deeper look revealed that students in individualized education programs (IEPs) had nearly no growth, and thus the achievement gap got bigger. So it seems that even innovative, successful schools are still leaving many children behind.

The picture across the country is not encouraging:

- In some of the most affluent districts, 20 percent or more of elementary students still read below grade level.
- In some urban districts, fewer than 5 percent of students with disabilities read or do math at grade level. That's only one of every twenty students.
- Nationwide, 64 percent of eighth graders struggle with reading.[2]

- Nationwide, only 18 percent of students living in poverty can read at grade level in fourth grade, and just 9 percent of students with disabilities can.[3]
- Perhaps the ultimate measure of performance (or lack thereof) in the knowledge-based twenty-first century is that only 27 percent of low-income students in 2010 met the ACT College Readiness Benchmark in reading, 16 percent in math, and 11 percent in science.[4]

YESTERDAY'S STRATEGIES AREN'T RIGHT FOR TODAY'S NEEDS

So why is the current system of supports not meeting the academic and social, emotional, and behavioral needs of struggling students with and without disabilities? Why are so many improvement efforts not really improving the situation? Because schools are still applying strategies that worked in the past, but today's needs are different.

In the seventies and eighties, two important trends were:

- An increasing number of students identified with disabilities
- A move toward greater inclusion

The practical solution at the time was:

- Add staff to handle the growing caseloads from greater identification of students
- Add paraprofessionals and co-teachers to ease the transition to including more students in the general education setting

These reasonable reactions to a changing need created the "add more" mind-set. It also deeply ingrained a special education approach to helping students into the psyche of school districts. Even when schools rolled out nonspecial education efforts like RTI and MTSS, many modeled the new efforts on the old special ed structures. Student

intervention team meetings for RTI often look like IEP meetings; identification of struggling general education students frequently looks like
IEP disability screening; much special education, like paperwork and
meetings, accompanies many MTSS efforts.

Today's challenges are different in three important ways:

- Schools don't have more students with disabilities, but they
  have many students with more-challenging needs. Over
  half (many more in urban districts) of struggling students
  don't even have disabilities. They just struggle to read or
  control their frustrations.
- Parents don't want just more inclusion, but more successful inclusion.
- District leaders don't want special education to be the
  solution, but they want general education, MTSS, and special education to be the answer.

These new challenges are also taking place in a very different context
from the seventies and eighties. The current era is one of much higher
standards; whether close reading of historic texts, explaining your
thinking in math, more demanding science and social studies requirements, or the demands of employers for a higher-skilled workforce,
more is expected from today's students than their peers of the past.

There is no longer a path to the middle class without solid reading, math, and thinking skills. Technical trades, for example, require
comprehending complex building codes and more than basic math. To
become an electrician, a person must study and master hundreds of
rules and regulations; welders are asked to find the midpoint of complex numbers like $33\frac{3}{8}$ or use the Pythagorean theorem in their work.
And, yes, they must also weld. Previously, just being a good welder
was enough to get hired, but not anymore. Additionally, most decent-
paying white-collar jobs require a college degree.

These higher demands on graduates come as more students entering
school are living in poverty, living with stress and trauma, and are thus

less ready to learn. Despite the greater demands, schools have tighter budgets. Adjusted for inflation, many districts are spending less per pupil today than before the Great Recession of 2007. Rising healthcare and pension costs are making it hard or impossible for districts to retain all their staff, even when the districts get a small increase in funding.

Given the new needs and challenges, a new approach is in order. How we serve struggling students must change. A new, commonsense plan for the twenty-first century is needed.

Fortunately, this is an upbeat story, despite the bleak backdrop. The six shifts in practice I propose can make a world of difference in the lives of students, teachers, parents, and taxpayers. These shifts in how schools serve struggling students with and without disabilities are both practical and affordable. They are common sense but far reaching. Most importantly, they are field tested and proven to work in the hectic, politically complex, underfunded world that is public education in the United States.

A THOUGHTFUL PLAN BASED ON THE THOUGHTS OF MANY

After a few years on the school board and a bit of soul-searching, I decided to change careers and tackle this challenge from the inside. I sold my manufacturing company and became a district administrator, hoping to become a superintendent soon after. I offered to work for one dollar a year if the Harvard, Massachusetts, Public Schools (no relationship to the university) would hire me as assistant superintendent for curriculum and instruction.

In all my research up to this point, this small suburban/rural district stood out most spectacularly. Students *with special needs* in this middle- to upper-middle-class community achieved at higher levels on state assessments than *general education* students did across the state. Kids with disabilities outperformed kids without disabilities. More surprising was that the Harvard Public Schools spent much less per pupil than most other districts in Massachusetts. The per-pupil spending was in the bottom quartile when ranked against other districts, yet the kids both with and without disabilities had higher achievements than all other districts in the state.

Within months of working in Harvard, I noticed many differences. Within a year, I understood what the schools did differently and why it was better. Soon after deciphering the magic that took place in the Harvard schools, I got an opportunity to see if these successful practices could be transplanted to another district. I was hired as superintendent in Arlington, Massachusetts. Like any good leader, I assumed the needs of struggling students would be a top priority. This turned out to be a huge understatement.

Two days before starting my new job, I got a call from the longtime special education director: "Hi, Nate, hope you enjoyed a little time off before starting here. We are excited that you are coming." The call started off cordially, even though I knew that many had concerns about a nontraditional, career-switching superintendent.

After a few more pleasantries, the special education director got to the real point of the call. There were a few things I should know, she offered: (1) the district had been accused of misrepresentation in its special education compliance reports for the last twelve years; (2) the state might withhold its IDEA funds as a result; (3) the commissioner of education himself wanted to meet with me to underscore the severity of the situation; and (4) the director was retiring effective immediately. I also learned, the following week, that the district had more formal special education complaints than 349 of the 351 districts in the state. I had walked into a real mess, which was also an opportunity.

I was up for a challenge, but what disappointed me was that all this storm and thunder was over compliance issues. No one seemed upset that too many students struggled to read and far too few students with disabilities went on to graduate from college.

I decided to use the threat of state action to revamp how we served struggling students and do it a breakneck speed. From the start, I knew I would have to partner closely with parents and the general education staff, because this work needed a lot of hands and much political cover.

The team in Arlington took a step back, honestly assessed its short-comings, studied what worked elsewhere, got tired of hearing me share the wonders of the Harvard Public Schools, and collectively updated the district's approach to serving students with special needs and other students who struggled. We embraced the six shifts in practice, which made all the difference. The results were impressive:

- The achievement gap between students with special needs and nondisabled peers closed as achievement increased. Proficiency rates climbed by thirty-nine points in ELA and thirty-three points in English at Arlington High School.
- The number of struggling readers K–5 decreased by 66 percent.
- The number of K–5 students who started the year behind in reading and achieved more than a year's growth rose from roughly 10 percent to 68 percent.

The Rennie Center for Education Research & Policy, Schools Matter national research, The Broad Center, and others validated these results. Additionally, causality was easy to confirm because two schools refused to adopt the reform efforts, and the results in both schools stayed flat.

In the end, a lot changed in Arlington, but nothing was radical or crazy or even high-tech. One observer put it best: "The approach was common sense, but not common place." The results were good, but the work was hard. A team approach made it all doable. (See the sidebar "It Takes a Team to Lead Special Education Reform in a District.")

I have since shared and implemented the six shifts far beyond Arlington, Massachusetts. I have spoken with many thousands of educators and worked directly with nearly two hundred districts in twenty-eight states. Along the way, I've refined the approach, learned how best (and how not) to implement the six shifts and engaged parents, staff, and students in creating a better future. The following chapters serve as a guide to updating RTI, MTSS, and special education for the new century.

IT TAKES A TEAM TO LEAD SPECIAL EDUCATION REFORM IN A DISTRICT

One of my first (of many) mistakes in improving special education came when I assumed that the special education staff and leadership would resist the changes I proposed. I assumed they would fight change because that's what most people do. Sure, I invited them into the process, but I didn't create the environment in which they could embrace and enthusiastically support the improvement effort.

I should have better appreciated that special education staff had incredibly hard jobs. They are asked to do a wider range of tasks than any other staff member. This includes IEP evaluations; writing IEPs; working with parents; teaching math, English, and reading; managing compliance; helping with behavior; and so on. The workload is too much for any one person. And they care deeply about the kids while juggling a near impossible workload.

My mistake was in trying to improve special education without their full partnership. I thought they would fight to hang on to the status quo. In truth, the special educators in Arlington were just doing what they had been trained and asked to do. I have since learned that many special educators, school psychologists, and others want to see things change and can be powerful allies in the reform effort.

A mistake at the other end of the spectrum, which I see often, is asking only the special education department to lead the improvement effort. Again and again, I witness the following sad scene: The annual ritual of the superintendent presenting the results of last year's state test to the school board. Slide after slide of graphs often revealing a large special education–general education achievement gap and painfully too few students with disabilities reading at grade level are flashed on a screen. At this point in the presentation, all the eyes in the room drift to the special education director, wondering what they are going to do to fix the situation. If students struggle to read, why aren't folks looking to the elementary principal? If students with special needs are behind in math, why isn't the math director the center of attention?

Students with disabilities and others who struggle are served by all educators and administrators, and it will take a team effort to implement the six shifts in strategy. The hard work requires an equal partnership between special education and general education, between principals and the central office, and between parents and the district. Quarterbacking this team effort must be the superintendent who sends the message that all kids are everyone's priority.

PAST REFORMS COME UP SHORT

Of course, no school or district has been ignoring low achievement and frustrated parents. Just the opposite is true. Districts have aggressively added staff, services, and spending to address the challenge. In most districts, even those with significant budget pressures, special education and MTSS budgets are growing. In one moderately large western district, for example, no matter how tight the budget, special education spending increased. Faced with draconian cuts in funding from the legislature, it had to cut nearly four hundred teachers. A hundred percent of the cuts were general education staff. At the same time, it increased special education staffing a bit (with no gain in achievement).

Over the long haul, schools have responded to inequity, the achievement gap, and growing social and emotional needs by adding staff and spending more: the number of special education staff has grown 19 percent since the 2000–2001 school year, and many more reading teachers and general education intervention math and English teachers have been added. [5] During the same years, the number of students served increased just 6 percent.

Before we debate about whether struggling students deserve more, let's reframe the question. Do they deserve better? Absolutely! Do they deserve more? If more helps, then yes, but it hasn't helped in the last two decades, and there is no reason to believe a few more full-time equivalents (FTE) will dramatically improve their lives. As a nation, we have roughly doubled spending on public education and added 138,000 full-time special education staff since 2000, and the results are still unacceptable. Doing a bit more of the same isn't fair or sufficient.

One last question worth asking and answering. Should we spend less? No, that doesn't help kids either. We need to spend, staff, and serve differently.

Fortunately, every idea, suggestion, or best practice in the chapters that follow is cost neutral. Districts can implement them within their current budgets. Funds will shift but do not need to be added. No longer must parents of students with special needs be pitted against those of students in general education: we can stop the scramble for limited resources and unite in a shared interest in excellent tier-one, general education classroom, instruction, effective interventions, expanded social emotional and behavioral services, and more effective and cost-effective special education.

LET'S HELP TEACHERS AS WELL AS STUDENTS

The need for a new plan to help struggling students goes well beyond spending and achievement issues. Our teachers deserve something different as well. Hard-working, caring, and passionate educators are losing heart. I'm saddened, as I talk to teachers across the country, by how exhausted they feel.

In an area of record spending and staffing, most special educators feel understaffed and overwhelmed. Why the paradox? Because more isn't helping. In every state, special educators are retiring early or leaving the profession. They are burned out. Young classroom teachers are also leaving the profession because they can't imagine another twenty-five years of problematic behaviors and struggling readers. Veteran teachers are retiring mid-year because even a few more months seems too much. Many districts struggle to hire special educators, speech therapists, or school psychologists, because too few graduates are entering the field. All fifty states and half of all districts report shortages in these fields.[6]

Staff frustration isn't limited to not having enough hands to do the work; staff are also exhausted by ineffective help. Across the state of Vermont, for example, a broad effort to improve MTSS (a good idea) has generated more teacher anger than thanks. For a multitude of well-intentioned reasons, the net effect of the state's effort was many hours out of the classroom for training, lots more meetings, and tons more paperwork, but few new ideas for helping struggling students and no gains in achievement. In many districts I visit, teachers refer to MTSS as a schedule of meetings and a raft of forms, sometimes with more assessing, but too seldom a valued tool to help them help their students. When good ideas are implemented poorly, they cease to be good ideas. Unfortunately, many RTI/MTSS efforts suffer from problematic implementation.

Perhaps a headline of the future might read, "Chronic teacher shortage due to influx of students with problematic behaviors." No trend since standardized testing has stressed teachers like the increase of emotional and physical outbursts in class. Every month, I hear stories of teachers and principals who consider leaving the profession because they are overwhelmed by this growing challenge. One remarkable, but not atypical, tale is that of a large district in Colorado. After a talk on best practices for meeting the social, emotional, and behavioral needs of students, I was approached by frustrated teachers and principals who shared their plans to retire or quit. "I just can't take it anymore," said one. "My husband insists I leave, I'm a wreck every night," said another, and a third lamented, "It's affecting my health and my sleep."

"Isn't the district taking steps to help?" I asked. "That was the last straw!" they all spat in frustration.

The district had taken action. Just that year it assigned a behavior coach to each school. While this at first seemed as if help was on the way, the effort, like the well-intended MTSS effort in Vermont, did more harm than good. A soon-to-retire principal shared one example that exemplified a good idea poorly executed. On the behavior specialist's first day in her school, the building leaders reviewed the seven most challenging students and asked the new behavior specialist to focus there first. The behavior specialist responded, "Sure I'll do my best, but these kids have some very significant needs. I don't have any training in behavior management, but I'll do my best. It's a bit overwhelming for me, but together hopefully we can make a difference."

It turns out that the district had just reassigned existing school psychologists to the job, hoping or assuming they had the needed skills and training. No one asked this particular school psychologist about her background. The school was disappointed, the principal demoralized, and the psychologist not very successful. Attrition was sure to follow. This frustrating, well-intentioned example is a case of rearranging, not reimagining, how to meet the needs of struggling students in the twenty-first century.

As school and districts adapt their approach to serving struggling students with and without disabilities, much must change. Schools and districts that have dramatically closed the achievement gap and prepared more students for success after graduation have done so by shifting from common practices to new best practices that are common sense, but not yet very common, including:

1. *Shifting from special ed to general ed.* Most struggling students spend a large part of their day in the general education classroom. Too often, the general education teacher assumes or hopes that special ed staff or intervention efforts will help their struggling students. While both can help, high-quality general education instruction is the bedrock of achievement for all students, especially those who struggle. Some classroom teachers will need help to hone their craft, but they are essential to raising achievement. Despite the importance of general education instruction, nationwide, students who struggle currently get less core instruction than their nonstruggling peers. The practice of disrupting core structure in reading and math must end.

2. *Shifting from more adults to more time.* Given the growing needs of students and stressed-out teachers, it's natural to think more staff will help, but it hasn't yet. Instead, students and teachers alike benefit from having extra time to master grade-level content. Core instruction is necessary, but not sufficient. Struggling students will also need extra time each day to learn skills from prior years, be retaught content that still puzzles them, be pretaught tomorrow's lesson, and unlearn misconceptions. This takes lots of extra instructional time but not lots of extra adults. Fortunately, it can also fit within the current school day.

3. *Shifting from generalists to specialists.* Who is teaching students matters as much (or more) than how much time they have

to learn. Struggling students need and deserve highly skilled teachers. In their quest to add adults, many schools can't afford certified teachers and instead rely on paraprofessionals. These hard-working, often underpaid folks care deeply, but they are not highly skilled teachers; they aren't even teachers. When certified special educators work with students, sometimes they bring deep knowledge and training in the content, but not always. A student who struggles to learn math, for example, needs a teacher fluent in math concepts and skilled at teaching math. The challenges are too varied for one superhero teacher to address them all. We should no longer expect special educators to be experts in the law; IEP evaluators; IEP writers; teachers of math, writing, reading; managers of behavior; advisers around autism; and trauma counselors. Staff should be allowed to play to their strength and specialize in areas of their choosing.

These first three shifts are interconnected and underpin best practices to raise academic achievement in students who struggle, with and without special needs, as depicted in figure 1.1.

4. *Shifting from deterrence to prevention.* The first three shifts can address the academic needs of students, the three "Rs" of the past, but not the fourth "R." Reading, writing, and arithmetic must be supported by a *readiness* to learn. Schools have the added task of addressing students' social, emotional, and behavioral (SEB) needs. As students have changed, so must our approach to school climate, mental health services, and behavior management. The past's focus on deterring problematic behavior with threats of punishment and addressing problems after they manifest works for some students, but a growing number of kids need more. For them, a focus on preventing outbursts, bullying, and the like before it happens is key.

FIGURE 1.1

The three interconnected shifts to raise achievement

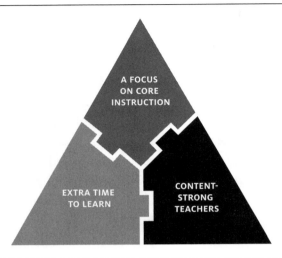

5. *Shifting from one good schedule to many great schedules.* The hours of the day are as precious and limited as dollars in the budget, but they aren't always managed as carefully. Providing extra time for intervention, not pulling students out of reading for speech and language, and not special education staff pushing into general education classrooms during critical whole-class instruction is important and logistically complex. Great schedules for schools, classrooms, and support teachers like special educators and interventionists are needed. Since these schedules are deeply interconnected, they must be built as a set through teamwork and guided by a shared vision of what is a great schedule.

6. *Shifting from managing compliance to managing practice, too.* As powerful and impactful as these shifts can be, they must be implemented well and at scale. Leaders and managers can't turn their backs on compliance; supporting teachers to do this well must be of equal (or greater) importance. Students and staff don't benefit from a good plan, only from a good plan well implemented. Better tools, systems, and organizational structures can supercharge doing the right stuff the right way.

Taken together, these six shifts can help students, teachers, parents, and taxpayers. By building on the past but being comfortable to reimagine a better future that dramatically changes how, who, when, and where struggling students receive help, we can transform the lives of our children with the greatest needs. Making this a reality won't be easy, but it's worth the effort.

One important side note: the six shifts have broad reach, including students struggling to read, kids with mild to moderate disabilities, English language learners, and children living in poverty. They will serve kids well in large districts and small, urban, suburban or rural, and across all social-economic ranges. That said, they aren't right for all children. They may not be best suited for many students with severe disabilities or with little or no English or prior schooling. And, of course, the I in IEP stands for individual, and some kids' needs will be unique.

CHAPTER 2

Shift #1: From Special Education to General Education

THE FIRST REQUIRED SHIFT in how schools and districts serve struggling students with and without special needs is a bit of "back to the future." Shifting from special education to general education harkens back to the long-known teaching and learning best practice that the classroom teacher matters, a lot.

Don't worry, special education isn't going away, but core instruction, general education, and gen ed interventions need to step up their game. School and district leaders need to help classroom teachers take on and excel at this added responsibility. To fully appreciate why shift #1, from special education to general education, is needed, a brief history lesson is in order.

The history of special education has been a long fight to help kids who needed more. In the 1970s, students with severe disabilities weren't even allowed in public schools, and parents were often left to fend (and pay) for themselves. President Ford ended this with the historic signing of the Education for All Handicapped Children Act, which was essentially the birth of special education in public schools.

The first students served by this groundbreaking legislation were children with severe disabilities, such as cognitive impairment, Down syndrome, and severe autism. These students could now attend school but went to special, separate classrooms. They were taught by special teachers as well, special educators to be exact. Over the next decade or two, students with learning disabilities, reading challenges, problematic behaviors, and other mild disabilities were also identified as qualifying for services under the special education laws. As the number of students with IEPs grew, the original concept of special rooms and special teachers lingered. For far too long, kids with disabilities were separated from nondisabled peers, and special educators played the lead role in their education. This separation was morally wrong and academically unsuccessful. The backlash to this over-reliance on substantially separate education gave birth to modern-day inclusion.

Through the 1990s and 2000s, more and more schools embraced inclusion, integrating and serving students with disabilities in the general education classroom. The hope was this would raise achievement, increase socialization, and create relationships among all children. Three ideas seemed to drive the push for inclusion:

- Students in substantially separate classes had low levels of academic achievement and dismal postgraduation outcomes.
- There was very little cross-socialization between students with and without disabilities.
- It just seemed morally wrong to shunt some students "to the basement" in often low-quality spaces with limited curriculum, aspirations, or expectations.

This reasoning helped guide the 1990 rewrite of IDEA, the updated version of President Ford's legislation and the 2001 No Child Left Behind (NCLB) Act. The first stressed educating students in the least restrictive environment, and the second called for assessing and publishing the results by subgroup, including students with disabilities. NCLB shined a light on the widespread low achievement of students with disabilities, even in overall high-achieving schools. The data screamed that substantially separate programs, classrooms exclusively serving students with special needs, ensured very little learning for many students. Inclusion became a North Star in schools across the county, sort of.

Few could debate the poor outcomes of many substantially separate programs, especially for students with mild or moderate special needs. The relatively better results in the forward-thinking first adopters of inclusion also helped the idea gain popularity. Federal requirements to serve students in the least restrictive environment further strengthened the push to inclusion. Despite the strong case for inclusion, many teachers and principals were scared by the concept. To be fair to them, virtually no school of education then (and few today) prepared general education classroom teachers for how to teach and differentiate instruction for students with learning differences.

It seems an unspoken, unwritten compromise was struck. It went something like this: okay, we will take kids with special needs into our discussion, but we need help. We will need specialists part of the day who understand these students, called "special education teachers." We will also need extra hands to help in our classes all day, called "paraprofessionals."

While much has changed since Gerald Ford signed his legislation, much has stayed surprisingly the same. Sure, *All in the Family* isn't a prime-time TV hit or "Silly Love Songs" by the Wings isn't at the top of the music charts, but the worry of many general education teachers and the idea that kids with special needs need special education teachers and paraprofessionals to teach them remain strong in many schools. Yes, inclusion is the norm and seldom debated, but too often it's "geographic inclusion." Kids are in the general education classroom, but still not primarily the responsibility of the general education teacher.

In 2019, many hundreds of classroom teachers in interviews all across the country shared with me that they don't feel equipped to meet the needs of many of their struggling students, especially those with disabilities, even mild disabilities, or reading or math challenges.

Fortunately, they quickly follow up by saying, "It's okay that I'm not an expert, because the special educators in my school are." With love, care, and high hopes, too many general education teachers pass responsibility for their students' success to special education to fix, remediate, and teach.

THE IMPORTANCE OF CORE INSTRUCTION, DELIVERED BY GENERAL ED CLASSROOM TEACHERS

The past practice of relying heavily on special educators and paraprofessionals raises the central question of shift #1, moving from special education to general education. Is it okay to keep this divide-and-conquer approach? Is it a problem that special educators are asked, and often accept, the charge of teaching kids with disabilities, especially mild to moderate disabilities?

Best-practice research and the demands of the twenty-first-century workforce clearly say we need to shift toward a much greater reliance on general education and general education core instruction, delivered by skilled classroom teachers to best serve students with mild to moderate disabilities and other struggling students. Special education still matters, but it can't be the beginning, middle, and end.

Both big data and small experiences prove the point. Education professor John Hattie's landmark review of educational research and many other studies show repeatedly that individual teacher effectiveness is the single largest school-based predictor of student learning and growth.[1] Sadly, a student's family income is still a stronger predictor, but among the variables school and district leaders can influence, teacher quality matters most. While this finding is widely known, an analysis by the Delivery Institute goes one step further, testing the theory specifically for students with IEPs.[2] The number-one predictor of achievement for students with disabilities is achievement of students without disabilities. This is true for a classroom, school, district, and even a state. The better core instruction is, the better students with and without an IEP will achieve. Figure 2.1 shows that in states with higher general education achievement, there is also higher achievement of students with special needs.

Mastering grade-level math and English at the secondary level has become a gatekeeper to higher education and higher earnings. Unfortunately, two-thirds of all students (not just those with special needs) at community colleges and four of ten of students at four-year schools

FIGURE 2.1

Comparison of special education and general education results of grade 4 NAEP reading by state

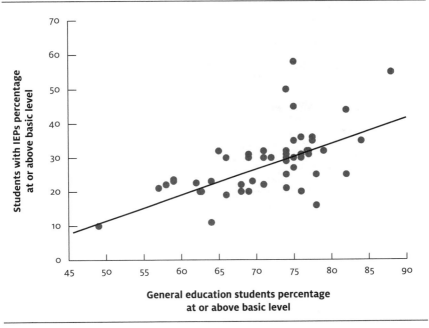

take remedial, noncredit-bearing courses at the start. This increases student debt and accelerates dropping out.[3]

On a far more anecdotal level, nearly every parent or principal can think of a classroom where nearly all the kids learn and grow at high levels: "Mrs. Jones is great with all kids, including students who struggle." A great classroom teacher can supercharge a struggling student's learning.

On reflection, this shouldn't be too surprising. Most kids with disabilities spend the bulk of their day with their general education teacher and only an hour or so with special education staff or related service therapists. It's unreasonable to expect to teach the current year's content and curriculum in an hour to kids who struggle, when kids who don't struggle need all day to master it. Figure 2.2 makes visible the

FIGURE 2.2

Distribution of a typical day for students with mild to moderate disabilities

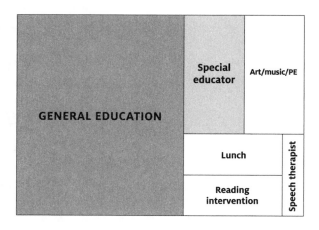

fact that general education teachers have most of the day to help, and special educators just a sliver.

The final reason that core instruction delivered by the classroom teacher is so important is the changing job market. After graduation, few middle-class jobs exist for earnest, hardworking, but poorly educated kids. Gone are the days when factory jobs, construction, or other "work with your hands" professions were open to kids who struggled to read, do math, or problem solve. These types of jobs still exist, but they require employees to work with their heads as well as their hands. Electricians must read and comprehend dense code books, factory workers do math-intensive statistical quality control, and many of these jobs now require at least an associate's college degree. The high standards that employers want are exactly what Common Core or other new state standards are designed to teach. This high-rigor instruction is being taught by the general education teacher every day, and struggling students with and without disabilities need to master it just as their nonstruggling peers do.

While the evidence is strong that high-quality, high-rigor core instruction helps, there is also mounting evidence that special education services, when overapplied, actually reduce outcomes. One study looked at kids on the bubble.[4] These were very similar students who got special education services in one school, but in another, didn't. Kids who got the IEP achieved like other students with disabilities, that is, they significantly underperformed their general education peers. Kids who might have received services elsewhere, but didn't get special education services actually achieved closer to their general education peers.

In more than a few schools, when general education takes the lead, referrals to special education drop, sometimes by as much as half. Reading achievement also rises (see the sidebar "Reading: The Skill to Rule Above All Others"). Teachers no longer view the referral as a golden ticket to coveted services. Strong core instruction paired with effective general education intervention often meets students' needs quicker, better, and more cost effectively than similar efforts within special education.

So, if core instruction matters greatly for student achievement and success after graduation, do most schools make this a priority for students with special needs? Yes, if you ask the principal, the director of curriculum and instruction, or the superintendent. Maybe, if you ask the classroom teacher. Some say yes; others sheepishly say no. Too many classroom teachers confess in private that they are counting on the special educators. The answer, however, is a resounding no if you look at student and staff schedules.

After working with more than 125 school districts across the country and analyzing more than fifty thousand special education staff schedules, it's clear to me that most students with disabilities (and other struggling students) get less core instruction than their nonstruggling peers. In most schools, kids who are having difficulty learning this year's content are frequently not in class to hear it, learn it, and process it. We shouldn't be too surprised that John didn't master third-grade math or fifth-grade writing, because he wasn't in the classroom when some of it was being taught.

READING: THE SKILL
TO RULE ABOVE ALL OTHERS

Core instruction is important, but not all core instruction is equally important. English language arts (ELA) and math are fundamental topics that spiral throughout grades K–12. Science, social studies, and world language are important, but not as important (no insult intended to science, social studies, or foreign language teachers). These other areas are important in the life of a well-educated student, but lacking a foundation in ELA and math makes learning the others very difficult. But above them all is reading. Reading is the gateway to all learning.

Difficulty with reading is a very common reason for a student to be referred for an IEP. Moreover, third-grade reading proficiency is a strong predictor of lifetime achievement. This works in both directions. Struggling third-grade readers seldom catch up and have difficulty reaching the solid middle class. Yet even kids living in poverty who read and comprehend well overcome the drag of poverty and graduate at rates similar to their wealthier peers.

There is a paradox when it comes to reading and special education. On one hand, everyone knows how important reading is. Teachers, principals, and district leaders can often quote the research chapter and verse. Schools invest heavily in the reading curriculum, reading professional development, and reading intervention. Many strategic plans include a goal for literacy.

How best to teach reading is well established. The National Reading Panel, the What Works Clearinghouse, and achievement-gap-closing schools all agree on a clear set of best practices, as summarized in figure 2.3.

Despite this widespread understanding of the importance of reading:

- Kids with disabilities get pulled out class during the reading lesson in roughly half the schools in America.
- By my informal count, only 5 percent to 10 percent of the schools in the one-hundred-plus districts I have studied implement the National Reading Panel and What Works Clearinghouse recommendations.
- Paraprofessionals provide much more reading intervention and support than certified teachers. In fact, reading help is the single most common task given to paraprofessionals. In many districts, two-thirds or more of reading support is provided by uncertified staff rather than skilled reading teachers.
- About two-thirds of elementary special educators have had no more than one class in how to teach reading, yet it is both a science and an art.

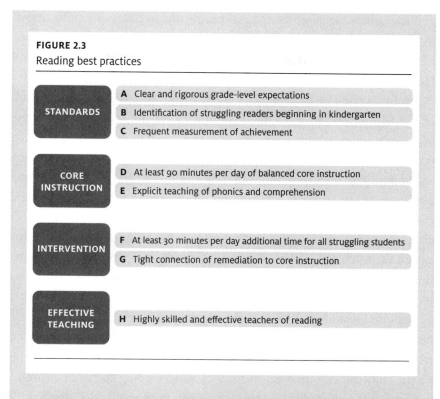

FIGURE 2.3
Reading best practices

STANDARDS
- **A** Clear and rigorous grade-level expectations
- **B** Identification of struggling readers beginning in kindergarten
- **C** Frequent measurement of achievement

CORE INSTRUCTION
- **D** At least 90 minutes per day of balanced core instruction
- **E** Explicit teaching of phonics and comprehension

INTERVENTION
- **F** At least 30 minutes per day additional time for all struggling students
- **G** Tight connection of remediation to core instruction

EFFECTIVE TEACHING
- **H** Highly skilled and effective teachers of reading

- Nearly all middle and high schools act as if all their students have mastered reading, especially comprehension and vocabulary. In many urban districts, half or more of their secondary students actually struggle with reading. These schools typically teach "English" that is reading to write and think, not how to read. The few that do teach reading too often have English teachers or special educators who lack training in teaching reading.

Ensuring that all students receive core instruction helps. Ensuring that core instruction prizes mastery in reading changes lives.

This shortchanging of core instruction for struggling students happens in two ways—on purpose and accidentally. In about half of the schools I visited, "extra" help for struggling students comes during core instruction. I remember observing in one classroom a strong, experienced teacher delivering an engaging reading lesson. She was sharing explicit comprehension strategies, specifically, five ways to make meaning from unfamiliar or unclear words or phrases. It was a great lesson. I hoped that every teacher in the district was teaching this skill and teaching it as well.

As I marveled at the teacher's craft, I noticed two girls in the back of the room playing "go fish." I assumed that they read and comprehended at such a high level that the teacher felt they didn't need to participate in the lesson. I understood not wanting to bore them but wondered why they weren't given a more challenging, growth-oriented alternative. The teacher, noticing my disapproving look (I'm a terrible poker player), quickly explained the situation. They were both struggling to read, she said, and they would be heading to the special education resource room in a few minutes. Since they wouldn't be able to finish most of the lesson on comprehension, there was no reason to have them start it, she explained. I couldn't hide my disappointment, so she quickly added, "I'm sure the special education teacher will work on comprehension with them." She didn't actually know this to be true, hadn't co-planned the lesson, but just hoped or assumed it to be so. In fact, the resource room teacher wasn't going to teach comprehension, but rather phonics, and worse yet, the special educator hadn't been trained in the five ways to improve comprehension. This was a textbook case of passing responsibility for a critical skill on to the special education department, even though the classroom teacher was best suited to teach it.

To be fair, most "passing of the baton" to special education isn't this explicit. It happens accidentally. More often, reading support is written into the IEP, and in many schools, special education teachers purposely try to schedule pullout—extra help in reading—during the core reading block. This way, everyone is getting reading instruction at the same time. This surgically precise pullout clearly isn't *extra* help, it's *instead of* help. The important takeaway here is that while core instruction is central to student success, many students who struggle aren't even in the room to participate in 100 percent of it.

ACCIDENTALLY MISSING CORE INSTRUCTION

In many other cases, however, kids with disabilities (or tier-two intervention needs) miss core instruction by accident, not by plan. Students with special needs often receive a number of services such as academic support and speech and language therapy. These supports have to happen sometime during the day, but when?

During many IEP meetings, the team spends much energy deciding how much service is needed. Thirty minutes a day or forty-five? Twice a week or three times? More is often assumed to be better. What they seldom discuss, however, is what the student will miss in order to receive these services.

The few times I have heard the question raised, the answer is often the vague promise, "We will do our best to minimize any loss of instruction." This is hope triumphing over reality. It avoids speaking the ugly truth: "Jose will miss some of math twice a week and some reading every day."

The other most common answer is, "Well, we have a policy not to pull from art, music, PE, lunch or recess, so don't worry. We care about the 'whole child.'" Again, this statement leaves unspoken the fact that Jose is almost certainly going to be pulled from core instruction.

Even when a special education teacher or a speech therapist wants to avoid lost core instruction, it just seems impossible to schedule all of the required services and see all the kiddos on their caseload without pulling some from core instruction. Scheduling constraints also drive lost core instruction.

(An important note: actually, it is possible to serve all the kids on caseloads without students ever missing a minute of core ELA or math or depriving students of electives and the arts. See chapter 7 to learn how.)

In most schools, pullout services reduce a student's access to 100 percent of core instruction, which undermines their learning. Whether this happens by plan or unavoidably and with regrets, it's still not beneficial. Figure 2.4 depicts how more help often becomes less core instruction.

FIGURE 2.4

Comparing schedules of students who struggle and students who don't

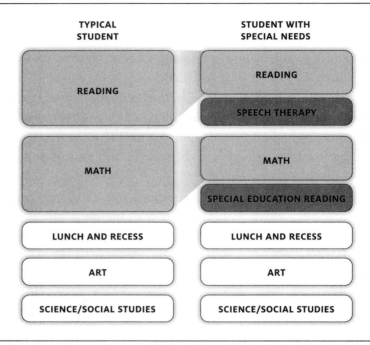

If the history and evolution of special education help explain how we got to the situation where general education too often takes a back seat to special education, why does this still persist today? Why do smart, caring teachers do this? The most common answers I've gotten are:

- "They have learning disabilities and that's not my expertise."
- "I'm not sure, but it's what we do it in this school."
- "They want it done this way." (On follow-up, staff can seldom remember who or when they were given this directive, but they are fairly certain this is the desired plan.)
- "It's in the IEP."

This last reason resonates powerfully with many teachers. Fear of noncompliance runs high. IEPs should serve the needs of students, not become obstacles to this goal. Some schools must bust the myth that the law mandates a greater role for special education. The law mandates that schools honor what's written into the IEP, but not what, when, and how to meet a student's needs.

A lunchtime conversation between two great elementary classroom teachers has always stuck in my head. Let's call them Mary and Sally. Both teachers achieve way above average student growth in reading. Year after year, they generate more than a year of growth for most of their students. Mary commented that the new special education teacher in the school seemed weak in teaching reading and was worried about a few of her students with IEPs.

"I feel guilty when they leave the room," she said. "I'm sure I could do a better job teaching them."

Sally interjected, "I never let my kiddos leave during reading or intervention time."

"Isn't that illegal?" Mary countered.

Sally replied, "Maybe, I don't really know, but I do it anyway. I just tell the special educator that she can't have them then."

"I wish I could, but I don't think we can," Mary lamented.

It's frustrating to see a bad understanding of a good law ultimately hurt the students it is intended to help.

HOW TO HELP TEACHERS MAKE THE SHIFT

The research is clear and achievement-gap-closing schools are resolute about the importance of core instruction, but general education teachers' concerns and hesitations are valid. Central to facilitating the shift from special education to general education is building the capacity and comfort of classroom teachers. This discomfort three decades ago was a root cause of today's challenge. Having classroom teachers take primary responsibility for all students, including kids with mild to moderate disabilities, is easier said than done. It's not that they don't want the responsibility; more often than not, they just aren't sure how to take that responsibility. This commonsense idea isn't commonplace due to a lack of will, but rather skill.

General education staff are taking primary responsibility for their struggling students when both their perceptions and actions change. Gone is the day when kind, caring teachers think that a paraprofessional is more likely to help a child to read than they are, or when they think special educators have some mysterious means of teaching content that they can never know. On a less theoretical level, it means that they won't let anyone pull students out of their class during core instruction in reading and math, that they will plan lessons that scaffold new material and reteach prior standards, and that they will guide interventions, even if they aren't delivering them. To see if your district can benefit from a greater role for general education in serving struggling students, take the self-assessment in the appendix at the end of the chapter.

Teachers in a statewide study in Vermont, for example, speak for their colleagues across the country when they say, for example, "I'm not at all sure what to do with students who struggle to read. I've taught the lessons and some students didn't learn. It makes no sense for me to teach it again, but I'm not sure what to do differently" or "Look, our special educators have all the training, not me. I was never taught anything about kids with disabilities. They are the experts, not me."

About a year later, I met with many of these Vermont teachers, and together we brainstormed how best to build their capacity to better serve struggling students with and without an IEP. The ideas shared included:

- *Dispel the myth that special educators have magic powers and mystical tools that they do not.* This is not meant to demean special educators, but to have classroom teachers realize that they aren't helping students when they back away. I've heard many general education teachers use the analogy, "I'm the family doctor and the special educator is the heart surgeon. A caring doctor naturally refers a patient in need to a specialist." So long as classroom teachers feel this is true, that special educators have a high skill level, as the heart surgeon, then their love for kids will discourage this shift in practice. Simply having general education and special education teachers in the same room for an open discussion about their respective training, coursework, and what happens in the resource room can help reset their understanding.

- *Identify general education teachers in each school who have made great academic gains with their students on IEPs.* Local proof points are much more compelling than national data. Many schools have highly effective teachers who are already making great strides for students with disabilities. They can help disprove the notion that only special educators can raise achievement.

- *Provide in-class, embedded, instructional coaching in the pedagogy of teaching students with learning challenges.* A few PD sessions won't be adequate, but sustained instructional coaching has been a very effective strategy for increasing teacher capacity. Research is clear. Skilled instructional coaches spending time in the classroom modeling lessons, observing instruction, and giving immediate honest feedback can change and improve teacher skills.

  Some special education teachers can make excellent pedagogical coaches. They have deep training in the methods of effective teaching, such as "chunking" (breaking a big idea down into small blocks of instruction), scaffolding (reminding of prior learning), and homework design (give a few targeted questions, not dozens of repetitive ones that test stamina more than ability).

- *Utilize master teachers.* The master teacher concept is another good avenue for effective coaching. Once you identify classroom teachers who are successful with all their students, including those that learn differently, appoint them as master teachers. Anointing a highly effective teacher to be a master teacher, often paired with a stipend, can free up and empower them to help their colleagues. They can lead professional learning community

(PLC) discussions and mentor novice teachers. In some schools, they leave their classroom for a few hours a week to support grade-level peers. During this time, another adult covers their class, such as a guidance counselor doing social emotional learning (SEL) lessons, a paraprofessional overseeing independent work, an art teacher providing an extra period of art or a parent volunteer supervising a technology-enabled personalized learning.

Some might feel it unfair that these students see their great classroom teacher for fewer hours each week, but isn't more unfair that other students have a less-skilled teacher every day, all day. Perhaps the greatest inequity in our schools is access to highly skilled teachers, especially those who can meet the needs of struggling students.

- *Embrace universal design for learning (UDL), but with a twist.* UDL is founded on the idea that effective general education teaching is impactful for struggling students and what's helpful to struggling students is awfully good for all other students. Thus, it's not surprising that many school or district leaders wanting to improve core instruction for all rush to UDL. I'm a fan, but surprisingly many teachers I meet are unexcited, maybe even slightly jaundiced, by the approach.

Their lack of enthusiasm stems not from a disagreement with the *concept* of UDL, but rather uncertainly over how exactly to implement it. Too often, UDL is explained in a few hours or a day of PD at the big-picture level. Then the teachers are left to figure out how to make it real every day. The PD moved the ball a yard or two, but then it's up to each individual to run the other ninety-nine yards down the field for a touchdown. What the teachers want is specific, concrete help applying UDL principles to their existing lessons, classroom activities, quizzes, assessments, and other daily elements of teaching. They want to do this as a group, led by an expert, culminating in creating physical artifacts to use in class.

The Vermont teachers had a lot of good ideas, supported by success from across the country. One idea to avoid is going gung ho on "differentiated instruction," the concept that a teacher delivers a lesson in multiple ways to meet the different needs of the students in the classroom. Some people love it; others believe it's impractical. Despite strong feelings on both sides, few can agree on a definition.

I'm not taking sides on this debate, but what I've learned from teachers who might be reluctant to take on the scary job of being primarily responsible for all their students is that UDL sounds doable—one way of teaching and assessing that will work for all my kids. "Okay, I can do that," they tell me. Too many teachers hear about differentiation and believe they need four lesson plans, two quizzes, and three homework assignments for each unit and immediately get overwhelmed. "I'll need two teachers, three paraprofessionals, and more planning time," they fuss. While this isn't actually what differentiation requires, its reputation and widespread misunderstanding can kill this shift before it starts.

PROCEED CAUTIOUSLY WITH PUSH-IN OR CO-TEACHING

I suspect that many readers who are advocates of push-in services (a teacher or paraprofessional helping out a few students in the general education classroom) or co-teaching (a special education and a general education teacher jointly leading a class) are feeling good about their preference. Both of these common IEP practices ensure students access to all core instruction. But do they really?

Push-in and co-teaching emerged as alternatives to pullout—substantially separate or replacement classes—in large part because of the above stated shortcomings of pullout, that is, less core instruction. The schools I visit that strongly embrace push-in or co-teaching they share this fact with great pride. They feel it is much better for kids. In theory, these in-class support strategies should provide better access to core instruction. Sometimes they do, but often in practice, they don't.

Often push-in or co-teaching creates an invisible barrier between the student with an IEP and their general education teacher. I'm reminded of Sue Storm from the *Fantastic Four* comic books of my youth. One of her powers, along with invisibility, is the ability to create a clear, nearly impenetrable force field around her and those near her.

Keeping in mind the prevailing belief that special education teachers do have superpowers, not force fields or invisibility, but the power to teach kids with learning disabilities, it's not surprising how often I witness a divide-and-conquer approach. General education kids are taught more by the classroom teacher, and the others by the special educator. This is especially apparent during small-group time or when a student has a question.

See if you can spot the reduced access to core instruction in this scenario. A student without an IEP asks a question. The classroom teacher pauses the lesson and answers the question for everyone. A few minutes later, a student with disabilities asks a question. This time, the special education teacher quickly and quietly moves to the student's desk and answers the question, providing one-on-one personalized support. Unfortunately, the classroom teacher doesn't stop the lesson. Since the student with co-teaching or push-in on their IEP can't listen to two people at once, she misses some of the whole-class lesson. If the struggling student is really confused or frustrated, the special education teacher might even do a mini lesson, trying to reteach past material. This is a good way to fill a skill gap but might also create a new gap in today's content.

Some flavors of push-in are actually a shunting of students to special education, but without having to leave the room. This can happen during small-group instruction. The special ed push-in or co-teacher pulls three to five students to the back of the room to work on specific skills or needs. Again, the rest of the class is learning today's content, but the three to five students are not. A better, but still not great variant is when the entire class breaks into small groups, the classroom teacher works exclusively with nondisabled students, and the special educator provides instruction exclusively to her kids.

Given the importance of kids accessing 100 percent of core math and ELA, it might seem logical that push-in or co-teaching is best, given the propensity of pullout to reduce time in class. Surprisingly most gap-closing schools have pullout, but meticulously schedule the pullout at appropriate times.

Additionally, another drawback of push-in or co-teaching is that this strategy doubles up on adults but doesn't provide students any extra time to learn. Few districts can afford staff for the both push-in or co-teaching and extra intervention or remediation time. Typically, an individual student gets one or the other, but not both. Chapter 3 will make the case that extra time to master grade-level content and skills is a must for most struggling students, including those with IEPs.

Oddly, the worst culprit in denying students 100 percent of core instruction and general education teachers taking primary responsibility for all their students is something highly sought after by classroom teachers, principals, and parents. This counterproductive strategy is the paraprofessional for academic needs.

To be sure, paraprofessionals play an important role in schools and provide many critical services to kids with disabilities and the class as a whole. But when they replace the general education classroom teacher, students do not benefit, no matter how widespread the practice. The presence of paraprofessionals in the classroom is increasing. Since 2000, schools have added 149,000 additional paraprofessionals, a 49 percent increase. In fact, there are now more special education paraprofessionals in the United States than special education teachers. Twenty years ago, special education teachers outnumbered paraprofessionals by 27 percent. Based on the latest data available, special education paraprofessionals now outnumber special education teachers by 24 percent.[5]

If you are thinking that in your school or district, paraprofessionals never replace the classroom teacher, but just help redirect kids, manage behaviors, and provide extra hands, think again. In one suburban district, I got into a heated debate with the principals after making a similar comment. Each proclaimed with energy and anger that they would never, *ever* have paraprofessionals substitute for the classroom teacher. Their certainty contrasted with my classroom observations, focus groups, and interviews. To settle the matter, we asked folks to do a time study for one week. The results shocked the principals.

- Seventy-five percent of paraprofessional time went to direct instruction, mostly one on one and mostly in reading.
- Twenty-five percent of special education teacher time went to preparing lessons for paraprofessionals to deliver while in the general education classroom.

Was this district an outlier? Based on scheduling-sharing studies from across the country, more than half of all paraprofessional time in elementary schools is dedicated to providing direct academic instruction. When the paraprofessionals are working with the students, the students are missing instruction from the classroom teacher. It's also understandable that a teacher with twenty-five students might feel OK that he focuses on twenty-three kids and the other two get very individualized help. This forgets that the quality of instruction matters most.

The principals' misunderstanding helped explained why, in their high-performing district, so many students with mild to moderate disabilities struggled to read or achieve at high levels. After abandoning this approach of paraprofessionals as stealth teachers, the number of struggling readers in fourth grade, for example, dropped by 25 percent. In a nearby district, which adopted a similar strategy, nearly 20 percent more students with disabilities achieved more than a year's growth. Classroom teachers providing and ensuring 100 percent core instruction were a big component of both these gains.

Self-assessment: Shifting from special education to general education

	MOST OF THE TIME	SOME OF THE TIME	NOT OFTEN	UNSURE/ NA
1. Are reading and math protected time with no pullout allowed?				
2. Are there formal written policies for when pullout can take place?				
3. Do classroom teachers answer most questions asked by students with disabilities during co-taught or push-in periods or when a para-professional is in the room?				
4. Do classroom teachers feel they are primarily responsible for the achievement of students with special needs?				
5. Do you honestly assess and survey classroom teachers' beliefs about their role serving students with mild to moderate disabilities?				
6. During co-teaching, does the general education teacher have small-group instruction that includes students with disabilities?				
7. Do you ask teachers about their skill and comfort in teaching students with learning disabilities?				
8. Do classroom teachers get pedagogical coaching at least a few times each month?				

CHAPTER 3

Shift #2: From More Adults to More Time

K IDS WHO STRUGGLE need 100 percent of core instruction, but need even more than this. Core instruction is necessary, but insufficient. The very definition of a struggling student is one who, after receiving core instruction, still hasn't mastered the grade-level content. Gone, thankfully, are the days when some schools just accepted the fact that some students hadn't mastered the material and moved on to the next chapter or grade. The critical question is "More of *what* will be most effective?" How can schools help the most kids catch up the most quickly?

The answer defines a district's theory of action for closing the achievement gap. This question is important for the lives of millions of struggling students, but it's seldom answered clearly and publicly. Despite lots of words on the special education pages of most district websites, little is written about what leaders think will raise achievement and change the lives of struggling students. These pages include lots of phone numbers, long lists of services and programs offered, usually some links to state laws and a guide to parents' rights, but not a theory of action for what it will take to improve outcomes for struggling students with or without disabilities.

All districts have a plan. Many theories of action are implicit, not explicit. By looking at the sum of a district's actions, one can infer the underlying theory that's driving these actions. For many schools and districts, their theory of action is in plain sight. If a visitor from another planet landed on Earth and strolled through almost any school in the United States, they would quickly deduce that some kids seem to need a lot more adults to help them learn than other kids do. Even without learning English (or any earthly tongue), they would figure out the most common theory of action for helping kids with disabilities. John, our Martian visitor, would astutely observe that most kids spend their day with one adult at a time, typically with about twenty-five other kids in the room. He would also see that a few other students interact with many more adults and often with only a few other students in the room.

While most classrooms have one teacher and twenty to twenty-five or even thirty students, some special kids get two teachers part of the day and at other times are paired with just three to four students at a time with another adult. Some fortunate kids get an adult just to themselves or with perhaps one other student. These other adults include paraprofessionals, special educators, school psychologists, speech therapists, and others.

If John the Martian had been to Earth before, he would have likely concluded that this strategy of lots of adults working with just a few kids must be very effective. Year after year, visit after visit, he has noticed that there were more of these extra adults in the schools, even when the number of kids didn't change.

Without ever declaring it publicly, most schools and districts have coalesced around a plan to raise achievement for students with IEPs and others who struggle. The plan centers on more adults working with fewer students at a time. The unstated theory of action is that if we reduce the adult-to-student ratio, then struggling students will get more attention and thus learn at higher levels. This de facto theory of action explains the steady increase in special education staffing across the country, even as the number of students with disabilities has plateaued.

The steady climb of special educator staffing didn't even abate during the tight financial times of the Great Recession. One large district facing draconian cuts in state funding laid off over four hundred general education teachers, while adding more than twenty special education staff at the same time. Another district facing a funding shortfall cut elementary art and music in half and reduced electives at the high school, yet still increased the number of special education paraprofessionals.

If all this extra staff, intended to help a group of kids needing lots of help, actually improved outcomes, we should celebrate thoughtful and heroic spending decisions by visionary, caring school boards. But let's be honest, during decades of ever-growing staffing, the special education–general education achievement gap has barely budged and, in too many districts, has actually gotten worse. The story for other struggling students isn't much different. Massive investments in RTI/MTSS teachers, tutors, and paraprofessionals has still left 63 percent of fourth graders in the country reading below grade level.[1] The objection to more staff isn't that it costs a lot, but that it's not creating the learning and achievement that students deserve. Few are satisfied with the stubborn achievement gap, and all districts are working hard to close it.

When I visit a district, I ask almost everyone I meet the same question: "If the district could do one thing to raise achievement of students with mild to moderate disabilities or who just struggle, what would you change?" The most common answer is "more staff. We need more paraprofessionals, more school psychologists, more co-teachers, and more special educators." The second most common answer is "more general education teachers to reduce class size so that the teachers can better personalize instruction." Nearly everyone interviewed feels more adults working with fewer students at a time will turn the tide. Oddly, this strong desire for more adults is unfaltering, even though the last twenty years of doing just this hasn't helped much.

There also seems to be nearly no limit to the desire for more adults. After completing a nationwide study of special education staffing that included more than 1,400 districts serving more than 10 million students, I visited a midsized district in the Northeast that had more special education staffing (adjusted for enrollment) than 99 percent of all other districts. It had more paraprofessionals, more special educators, more related services, more everything than nearly anywhere else. In over one hundred interviews, everyone agreed that more staff was needed. One administrator summed it up this way, spitting in frustration, "It's unreasonable to think we can serve our students well if we can't get a lot more staff!"

It's easy to understand why nearly everyone wants more adults and smaller groups. No caring person could argue that the status quo is good enough. Something needs to change, and it would be crazy to think that fewer adults and larger groups would be better for kids. So, if more adults in ever smaller groups aren't the answer, what should schools and districts do instead? Shift from a focus on more staff to a commitment to more instructional time. And don't forget that the classroom teacher's strong core instruction is still the foundation on which this extra time is added.

Students who struggle need more time to learn. Educational researcher Richard DuFour said it the best, "Time should be the variable and learning the constant." This means that some kids will need more time to learn each day than some of their quicker-learning peers. It's a form of differentiation. Some kids will have different schedules providing more or fewer minutes of instruction in a given topic.

At the elementary level, the extra time to learn is typically focused on mastering reading. For example, the district I led, Arlington, Massachusetts, created the "Reading Guarantee," a binding promise to parents and kids. All struggling readers, with and without an IEP, who didn't reach benchmark proficiency were automatically entitled to at least thirty minutes of extra reading instruction each day. If they fell further behind, they would automatically receive an extra hour a day of reading instruction until they caught up. No special evaluations, no lengthy planning meetings, just immediate action. Extra time to learn was a right, not an option. To underscore the obvious, the extra time truly was in addition to core instruction, not instead of or during core instruction. The results were heartening. Reading proficiency rose from 76 percent of students to 92 percent in just three years. It climbed a bit higher in the years that followed, as shown in figure 3.1. Perhaps even more importantly, most students who started the year behind achieved more than a year's growth, thus closing the gap. Before the extra time

FIGURE 3.1

Gains in reading achievement based on extra-time model

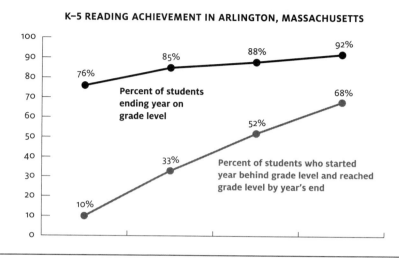

K–5 READING ACHIEVEMENT IN ARLINGTON, MASSACHUSETTS

and the 100 percent effective core model, roughly 90 percent of students who started the year behind ended the year further behind.

The Arlington schools' experience makes for a compelling tale. When shared as a concept, extra instructional time for struggling students is usually well received initially. Teachers and principals alike say things like, "Sure makes sense, let's do it." Quickly thereafter, reality dumps buckets of cold water on the embers of this idea.

The pushback starts fast and snowballs from there. One prototypical district in the Midwest went from excited to oppositional in about a week. "We would have to lengthen the school day, which will anger parents, mess up transportation, and blow the budget," said one panicked principal. Another shared that his art and PE staff had organized a schoolwide revolt against denying children a well-rounded education, and the special education director warned of widespread noncompliance, hefty fines, and maybe even incarceration for the superintendent. Yes, she really said this.

To be clear, no one had ever suggested that the school day be extended, that kids should miss art, or that IEPs be ignored. All this anxiety and fear stemmed from a false assumption that extra instructional time would be shoehorned into the current schedule, rather than creating a school day that built in extra-time intervention for some from the start. The district had to reimagine the school day, not shove extra learning time into an already full schedule. Achievement-gap-closing districts are rethinking their schedules and providing struggling students extra time, without lengthening the school day or ignoring the arts.

AT THE ELEMENTARY LEVEL

In Arlington, we set out to build a schedule that embraced extra time to learn for those who needed it. With the help of a skilled scheduler, the district created a schedule in each school with a daily thirty-minute intervention and enrichment block. To find the time in a previously full day, it integrated the formerly separate social studies period into the existing ELA block. This meant incorporating independent reading books at various levels of complexity and whole-class read-alouds that were tightly connected to the grade-level social studies standards. It also meant that half the book reports and many other writing assignments were also tied to the social studies curriculum. We didn't add more writing assignments or more time to read, but we did substitute some of the prior assignments to teach social studies, reading, and writing at the same time.

Kudos go to the district social studies director not only for mapping the integration and helping select the books and assignments, but for seeing the big picture. Rather than fighting the reduction of social studies time in the schedule, she viewed the change as good. She summed up her thinking like this: "I want all kids to love learning, crave history, and ultimately take AP social studies courses. Any student who can't read and comprehend well will never do any of these things. In the long run, improving reading ability today improves social studies mastery tomorrow." Sadly, too often, departmental turf wars get in the way of providing extra time to those who need it.

Beyond creating time in the schedule, the district also methodically ensured that IEPs were rewritten with parent and IEP team permission to facilitate special education reading supports to take place during the intervention period. Art, PE, and music were unaltered, so there was no need to panic about not valuing the whole child (which the district valued greatly). The schedule also incorporated common planning time so grade-level teams could plan intervention efforts together.

Teaching the extra-time interventions was a collective effort, not just for special educators and the classroom teachers, but both these roles and more. Reading interventionists and Title I teachers also helped provide the extra-time instruction.

While all teachers wanted small groups during this extra time intervention, the district fought off the siren call of small groups and instead embraced grouping by student needs and teacher strengths instead, including:

- All classrooms at a given grade level had their intervention and enrichment block at the same time of day.
- All special educators, ELL teachers, reading teachers, and interventionists were assigned to support the grade level during this period as well. They called it "flooding" the grade with staff.
- By staggering each grade's intervention block, all six grades could be flooded at different times during the day. The flooding required three hours a day from each special education and other support teacher, leaving ample time for all their other responsibilities.
- This created a pool of four classroom teachers, two special educators, one Title I teacher, and one reading teacher, all free at the same time. So, there were eight staff to help a group of a hundred students.
- Students, regardless of whether they had Mr. Jones or Mrs. Smith for homeroom or whether they had an IEP or not were placed in a group targeting their most-pressing need. One group might focus on phonics, another on comprehension, yet another

on fluency. If lots of kids had a similar need, two more targeted groups would be formed, one for phonics of consonants and the other for phonics of vowel sounds. One or two enrichment groups were also formed. These tended to be larger than the intervention groups. In all, eight groups were created. Typically, new groups were reformed every four to eight weeks.

- Groups were based on common formative and benchmark assessments, and no additional testing, paperwork, or meetings were required. Careful progress monitoring drove regrouping as appropriate.
- Teachers, regardless of their title, class roster, or caseload, were assigned to groups that emphasized their strength and expertise, not title. One classroom teacher who was skilled in teaching phonics would get a group of students struggling in phonics. The students came from any classroom. A special education teacher, skilled in teaching decoding, led the group struggling to decode, and so on.
- During common planning time, the teachers created these thoughtful intervention group assignments.

An alternative approach is having a cadre of skilled reading teachers pulling out kids (not during reading or math) for tier-two intervention throughout the day. A full-time reading teacher can be expected to support about eight groups of five students each day.

This very successful example underscores the point that what happens during the extra time matters as much as having the time itself.

AT THE SECONDARY LEVEL

Middle and high school students who struggle also need extra time to learn, more time than elementary students, but the practice is much less common. Why is there a greater need at the secondary level?

Think of an eighth or ninth grader struggling in math. They were unlikely to have started to struggle on the first day of eighth or ninth grade. More typical is that they have struggled for some time and have skill gaps and misunderstandings dating back to sixth and seventh grade. In some cases, the struggle is a weak grasp of foundational concepts like fractions and number sense—concepts first taught and assumed to be mastered in elementary school.

If these students don't get extra instructional time, then when will they master these key prior-grade skills that underpin higher-level math? It's unrealistic that an eighth- or ninth-grade math teacher would stop a class and spend considerable time reteaching fifth- or sixth-grade material that only a few students haven't already mastered. Unfortunately, the teacher is already feeling rushed for time trying to cover this year's content. There is no time to teach the prior year curriculum.

Beyond the need to teach prior skills and content, some struggling students simply learn at a slower pace. My three children have learning styles (and speed) that are completely different. One child can hear new content, grasp it immediately, and be ready to move on in minutes. Another needs time to process, question, revisit, and digest it over a few days. Both are strong in math, but one is faster to learn.

The extra instructional time model is a boon for kids like my second child. Remember DuFour's proclamation: "Learning should be the constant and time the variable." During the extra instructional time, current-year material can be pretaught, retaught, discussed, and ultimately mastered. Why do we think 100 percent of eighth graders will master eighth-grade math in forty-five minutes a day? Common sense tells us that some would need more time, others less, but it's not common practice to give some kids more time to learn.

The preferred approach of the achievement-gap-closing schools I have studied and the published research suggest that a double-block model of extra help for students is powerful, as depicted in figure 3.2.

In this approach, struggling students, with and without an IEP, get 100 percent of current-year core instruction by attending the regular, grade-level math and English classes with their nonstruggling peers. They also attend an extra period of math, ELA, or reading support every day. This provides double the instructional time in their subject of

FIGURE 3.2

Extra-time model for secondary schools

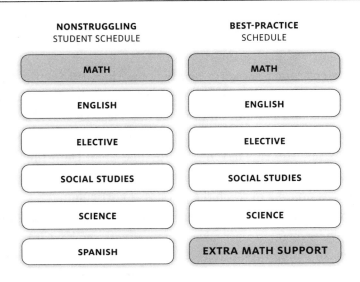

FIGURE 3.3

Extra help but not extra time schedule

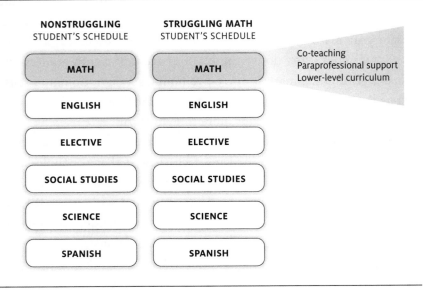

greatest need. This means 180 extra periods of instruction a year to fill skill gaps from prior years or repeat the lesson from the previous week that is still foggy in a student's head. This double block contrasts greatly with more typical efforts to help that try to shoehorn in extra help during the core period. This can take the form of two adults or a less rigorous curriculum, as depicted in figure 3.3.

In focus groups with teachers of these double-block classes, I learned that their biggest complaint is they have just one period a day to make up for so many years of prior learning. There is much to reteach and preteach, and it takes time to address a multitude of skill gaps and clear out the confusion that accumulates over the years. If these teachers feel rushed, imagine the plight of classroom teachers who are racing to cover the current year's content. When could they possibly remediate and intervene?

Shifting to the double-time model has created impressive gains for struggling students, as figures 3.4 and 3.5 indicate.

The most challenging case is when a student needs help in multiple subjects. Even King Solomon would struggle with this. It's tempting to split the time, say half English and half math—an extra ninety periods a year for each. In my experience, that's not enough time to catch up in either subject. Disillusionment sets in. One period a day seems like a lot, but by middle and high school, the prior skill gaps are also lot. In fact, some schools with longer days, like charter schools, provide two to three hours of intervention in a single subject each day. Rather than splitting the baby, I recommend letting the student select the topic they feel is their greatest need and focus on that every day for a year. Then, the next year the student is ready (and excited) to switch the topic of intervention. Also keep in mind that the lesson from the King Solomon tale was *not* to split the baby.

For students struggling in ELA, the added challenge is that ELA is one department in most secondary schools but two topics—writing and reading. Some kids need help with putting words on paper, and others struggle with comprehension. While connected, they are very different needs. Districts should be careful not to confuse or conflate

FIGURE 3.4

Rising achievement for students with disabilities in high school ELA

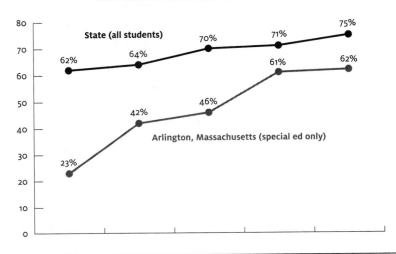

FIGURE 3.5

Rising achievement for students with disabilities in high school math

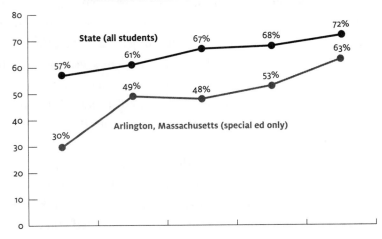

the two. Direct instruction for one is very different from the other. As such, many middle and high schools need to provide extra time for three subjects—reading, writing, and math.

Unfortunately, too few secondary schools offer direct instruction in reading. One data-driven urban school system in Pennsylvania, the school district of Lancaster, measured almost every aspect of a student's achievement (or lack thereof). It knew definitively that 48 percent of middle and high school students struggled to read. When the superintendent was asked what the system did for these kids, he looked puzzled and mumbled, "I guess we teach them to read?" When pressed for details, he lamely offered that he guessed special ed did this. A quick call to the special ed director revealed that only 18 percent of students had IEPs, so clearly, the system wasn't teaching all 48 percent of kids anything, and in fact, few of the special educators had any training in teaching reading. Most academic support was in the form of a resource room that focused on homework help.

Grasping for a better answer, the superintendent suggested, but didn't really believe, that English teachers provided instruction in reading. A poll of English teachers revealed that, yes, many of their students struggled to read the books they were assigned, but, no, they did not teach reading comprehension, fluency, or the like.

Shocked by this gap and creating the mantra, "If kids can't read, at any grade level, then we need to teach them to read," the district launched double-time scheduling with gusto. Every schedule was redesigned, staffing shifted, and extra help in reading, math, and English became the norm. Over the next few years, achievement soared. Dropout rates declined by 63 percent, and the district was honored by President Obama at the White House as one of the fastest-improving urban districts in the country.

"I DON'T FEEL STUPID ANYMORE"

One of the most common concerns about double time—extra instruction in middle and high school—is the fear of students becoming disengaged, cutting school, or even dropping out. One guidance counselor reflected the thinking of many: "If a student who struggles in math is forced to take lots of math and miss, say, art, the very thing that makes their day, we have hurt, not helped them."

The concern is well placed but assumes a lot. First, most kids don't hate math. They hate failing math, feeling confused, or struggling in math. Second, when giving up something, let's not take away what students love. If a student loves art, don't deny them art. Equally important, don't assume that all students really enjoy all of their noncore classes. I, for one, would have loved to skip music.

In interviews with students taking extra-time classes, I regularly hear and observe true excitement. "I finally don't feel stupid," said one. "It's starting to make sense to me now. It doesn't give me a headache anymore," said another. In fact, in one school, kids were sneaking into the extra-time class because they had heard from their friends how much it helped them catch up.

BUT WHAT ABOUT GROUP SIZE?

The desire for small groups does seem to push aside the need for more instructional time. The belief that small-group instruction matters a lot can drive schools to limit extra help to just a few kids, not everyone who needs it. So how many students should be in these extra-time classes and sessions?

At the elementary level, both the What Works Clearinghouse and the National Institutes of Health (NIH) reported no meaningful difference in outcomes in groups of one versus five students. The RTI action network recommended tier groups of five to eight students. Most of the achievement-gap-closing districts I've worked with target four or five elementary students with similar needs in a group.

At the secondary level, gap-closing schools typically have about fifteen to twenty students with like needs in a room. These figures are close to double what is typical in schools with stubborn achievement gaps. Once again, effective teachers providing targeted and direct instruction matter a lot; the number of kids in the room with this great teacher is not as important.

At this point, hopefully, you may be thinking, "Makes sense, kids who struggle need some extra time to learn . . . both current and prior year material." Perhaps you are also thinking, "Pretty obvious, not very imaginative for a book promising to reimagine special education."

But a review of over fifty thousand schedules of special educators, interventionists, reading teachers, and paraprofessionals from roughly 125 districts suggests that extra time might be common sense, but it's not common practice. The most common form of support is extra adults, not extra time. Moreover, while the groups working with the adults are typically small, very small in fact, they are seldom grouped by like area of need.

DON'T CONFUSE EXTRA-TIME LOOK-ALIKES

Extra instructional time for struggling students isn't a completely new concept. I suspect many might be thinking, "Yup, we've got this one covered already." Some schools are already providing this valuable gift to their students who need more time to learn. From the one-hundred-plus districts I've visited, roughly 50 percent provide extra time to kids with IEPs, and a smaller percentage for kids without IEPs. Unfortunately, many schools have the form of extra time but not the substance. Their approach falls short of the best practices. Some of the most common pitfalls to avoid include the following.

Don't ration extra time to learn

Extra instructional time should be a right, not limited by the availability of staffing. In more than a few schools, reading teachers provide extra help in reading, for example, but is limited to just twenty to forty students in the school. This help is not available to all students who need the extra time and help. When I visit these schools, the principal often shares, "Look, we have just one reading teacher, and she can help just twenty to thirty kids; any more would drive up her caseload." If reading recovery is the intervention of choice, typically far fewer kids are receiving extra time.

The principals in many schools bemoan the Sophie's choice of which kids to help. Some focus on just the early grades; others wait until grade two; some target just the bottom 10 percent of kids or those who didn't get extra time the year before. These are not good choices. All kids who need extra help and time should get it.

Don't skimp on the extra time

One seemingly easy but counterproductive solution to rationing limited staff availability is to reduce the daily support to every other day, thus doubling the number of kids who can be served. Unfortunately, five days a week, thirty minutes a day in elementary school and nearly an hour a day in secondary school is the minimum. More is OK, but less won't typically be enough to help kids catch up to grade-level mastery.

Don't confuse replacement time with extra time

If a pullout session is, say, thirty minutes long, but is scheduled during core reading or math, then it's not extra time; it's just "instead of" time.

Don't let purchased programs drive the extra help

One principal joyously shared that his school used Title I money to buy a new phonics program for use during elementary intervention time. While the program was solid, and some kids certainly would benefit from it (those who struggled in phonics and phonemic awareness), it wasn't the best use of learning time for kids with decoding, fluency, or vocabulary needs.

Don't confuse the resource room with targeted extra instructional time

One of the most common forms of extra time for students with disabilities is the resource room. In this common practice, typically four to eight kids work in the resource room with a special educator (and/ or paraprofessional) to address IEP goals.

Because the I in IEP stands for *individual*, each student in the resource room has different IEP goals—math, phonics, and fluency, executive functioning, writing, social studies, and so on. Unfortunately for these diverse students, no teacher can simultaneously deliver eight different lessons at once. So rather than thirty or sixty minutes of direct instruction, the teacher splits his or her time into a few short one-on-one mini lessons, homework help, and quiz prep. The students often receive just a few minutes of direct instruction and have a supported study hall for the rest of the time.

Don't treat students with disabilities worse than their nondisabled struggling peers

No one would intentionally treat a student with a disability worse than a student without special needs, but historic practices in many schools lead to this unintended consequence.

Let's compare two struggling students in seventh grade, Alice and Jose. Alice doesn't have special needs; Jose does. Both are struggling primarily in math and have similar skill gaps and needs. Alice is scheduled for the math lab in her school, an extra-time intervention course taught by a math teacher. The class preteaches the current month's content, reteaches last month's, and teaches missing skills. This aligns nicely with the best practices, as it is direct instruction and is in addition to, not instead of, the core seventh-grade math class.

Jose, on the other hand, per his IEP, is scheduled for the resource room, the most common form of extra time for students with disabilities. The stated goal is to provide support for Jose in meeting his IEP goals. From a distance, this seems sensible, but after you spend an hour sitting in the back of the room, the shortcomings became clear.

There are seven students in Jose's class, and one paraprofessional assisting a special education teacher. While all the students are seventh graders, their IEP goals and needs differ greatly. Two students have study skills goals, one has goals in English, two have goals for math, another for reading, and the seventh has an all-encompassing "academic support" goal. So, how does one teacher simultaneously teach math, study skills, writing, reading, and "everything." She doesn't, because no one can. Watching the entire forty-eight-minute class, one observes seven students doing homework, asking a few questions of the teacher or paraprofessional, and the teacher spending about five minutes huddled beside each student checking in and seeing how they are doing with their homework, big projects, and life in general. Not one minute is spent on direct instruction in preteaching or reteaching current content or prior skills gaps. Alice will likely catch up, but Jose is more likely to fall further behind.

The special education resource room is so deeply embedded in many districts, few in the schools can see its shortcomings. I remember when a special education teacher, I'll call her Sarah, asked me to observe her teach. She was proud of her twenty years in the system and was certain I would appreciate what she did for her students. Sarah was a committed, hardworking professional who gave every student her best. As I sat in the corner of the resource room for the afternoon, two thoughts kept passing through my mind:

- Will I see even one minute of direct instruction?
- How do I tell Sarah this time was not very helpful to her students?

After I observed for a few hours, thankfully the day ended, but Sarah wanted to debrief. Honesty trumped discretion, and I shared that all I saw was homework help and friendship, but not teaching or learning. She was hurt and tearful.

A few days after my visit to her classroom, she came to see me at my office, a meeting I dreaded. She began by thanking me for taking the time to visit her class. No superintendent or principal had ever observed her in the last twenty years. She also said, respectfully, tears starting to come again, that her feelings were very hurt. I quickly tried to apologize, but she cut me off. She continued, "Yes, I was hurt and mad. I went straight home and shared the story with my husband. He grew silent, however, and looked down at his feet. As I started to list all the ways I felt underappreciated, my husband stopped me and said, 'I have always wondered how you could teach five subjects at once? Especially math, you hate math and aren't very good at it. Sorry, but I've been thinking this for years, but was afraid to say it.'"

Sure, Sarah didn't talk to her husband for two days, but the story had a happy ending. She saw, for the first time, what an impossible task she had and became a key player in the district's reform effort to ensure extra instructional time, in topic-specific classes, from teachers strong in the subject.

Over time, she realized extra-help classes can't be multi-topic, but they can include students with and without disabilities. What mattered most was that all the kids get extra time to learn and have similar academic needs. As simple as this sounds, many schools don't target the extra help by topic.

LETTING GO OF PAST PRACTICES

In the last twenty years, *push-in* and *co-teaching* have become popular, even cherished, by special educators, general educators, and parents alike. Schools that have embraced co-teaching often beam with the pride of a parent showing off their child's straight A report card or championship baseball trophy. Given the bleak history of how schools served students with special needs in the years before inclusion became more widely embraced, I can easily understand the passion for these inclusive practices. Go back far enough in time (sadly, still true in a few districts today), and students with mild to moderate disabilities were relegated to substantially separate classrooms or pulled out of core instruction for special education math, special education reading, and other less rigorous replacement instruction. As a nation, we ultimately recognized this was ethically suspect and academically unsuccessful. Rigor and content-strong teachers were more often in the general education classroom, and that's where most struggling students belonged, including students with IEPs. My proposed shift #1 makes the case why this was a good start and an improvement over the historic practice of separation.

While a step forward, simply moving kids back into the general education classroom wasn't enough. General education classroom teachers at the time expressed great concern that they felt ill-equipped to teach such a heterogeneous class. This shouldn't have been a surprise, since they didn't really have much training in how to teach kids with disabilities. Teacher prep programs didn't cover this, and differentiation and UDL weren't widely discussed at the time either. Only 37 percent of elementary and special education teacher prep programs are explicitly teaching how to teach reading in accordance with published best practices such as the What Works Clearinghouse or National Reading Panel.[2]

A seemingly logical solution to the desire to include kids in general education and the teacher's hesitation was co-teaching or push-in services. Special education teachers and special education paraprofessionals would also move into the general education classroom along with the students with special needs. This took three common forms:

- A paraprofessional to help focus and support one or two students
- A push-in special educator to work with two to three students as needed during a lesson
- A special education co-teacher to jointly instruct the entire class, students both with and without disabilities

Partnering with the general teacher, all three forms provided more adults in the classroom. Certainly nothing negative could come from more inclusion and more adults, right? Actually, a lot of unintended consequences started to pop up, based on my conversations with more than a thousand co-teachers, push-in special educators and paraprofessionals, and hundreds of classroom observations. To be clear, inclusion is a best practice as embraced in shift #1, but too often schools created mostly geographic inclusion, not meaningful inclusion.

Far too often, two or more adults in a classroom utilize a divide-and-conquer approach, creating a special education bubble within the general education classroom. What does this look like?

- When a student with special needs has a question, the special educator or paraprofessional, but not the general education teacher, most often provides the help.
- When small groups are formed, kids with disabilities work with the paraprofessional or special educator, but seldom the classroom teacher.

Why is this a problem? For a few reasons. Inclusion is as much a social goal as an academic one, but these typical grouping practices reinforce separation. I visited a classroom in a district that was deeply committed to inclusion. When the teacher instructed students to work in pairs, a child with a mild disability turned their desk to the left to face a classmate, but the paraprofessional gently swung the desk to the right, back to her, and said, "I'll be your partner." Geographic inclusion was on full display.

Equally worrisome is that when a student without a disability has a question, they raise their hand, and the general education classroom teacher (perhaps assuming many other students have a similar question) pauses in sharing new content and explains and reteaches the entire class. Too often, however, when a student with a disability in a co-taught or push-in classroom has a question, the special educator huddles beside the student, sometimes bringing in one or two other students with IEPs, and teaches a quick mini lesson. This is reteaching or filling skill gaps in action. Unfortunately, it's also problematic because core instruction is continuing for the rest of the class. The struggling students are missing part of the day's lesson and will likely struggle with their homework. Perhaps the most problematic aspect to push-in and co-teaching is that it can preclude schools from utilizing the highly effective, extra instructional time strategy.

Co-teaching and push-in are expensive. Having two teachers in one classroom costs twice as much as one teacher. Based on a review of schedules from more than a hundred districts across the country, I've found that most schools that fund a second adult during core instruction don't also have funds for a teacher during the extra instructional time period. In theory, a school could offer two adults during core instruction and then one adult for an extra period as well, but in practice, financial reality forces a school to choose one strategy or the other. If only one strategy is possible, then extra time is the best choice for most struggling students, including those with mild to moderate disabilities.

Some of you may be offended by this last statement. I intend no offense. I understand and sympathize with the supporters of co-teaching and push-in. It's morally and ethically better than the past practice of separation and low rigor.

When co-teachers really gel, co-plan, and teach as equals, great things happen for students—all the students in the classroom. (See the sidebar "Great Co-Teaching Is Possible, but Difficult" for tips on supercharging co-teaching.) But the exception can't be the rule. John Hattie's landmark study of what works in education isn't very encouraging.[3] He determined that co-teaching, on the whole, had a 0.19 effect size. To put that in perspective, a 0.4 (twice as high) is considered to equal one year's growth over the course of a school year. Co-teaching, on average, leads to significantly less than a year's growth each year, which is a low bar for struggling students. They need to make more than a year's growth to catch up to grade level; thus, 0.19 is indication of an effective, perhaps regressive, approach. For another point of comparison, at the top of Hattie's list, scoring 1.57 is collective teacher efficacy, and RTI comes in at a strong 1.29 effect size.

In hundreds of interviews with general education co-teachers, many have shared that they delegate the primary responsibility for kids with mild to moderate disabilities to the special education teacher partner. Many special education co-teachers shared that they are disrespected and treated like a "glorified paraprofessional" by the general education teacher. While some great co-teaching partners are hitting it out of the park for kids, at scale it's been hard to replicate success, and unfortunately co-teaching usually reduces opportunities for extra instructional time to master grade-level material.

One extensive study observing two teachers in middle school classes found that 86.5 percent of the time students were engaged in whole-

GREAT CO-TEACHING IS POSSIBLE, BUT DIFFICULT

The promise of co-teaching seems alluring. The best of both worlds. Content expertise from the general education teacher paired with pedagogical expertise of the special educator, and two talented adults to facilitate small-group instruction. When it happens, it is a great situation for kids, but it doesn't happen very often. Why is it so rare?

- The two teachers need to have good chemistry, but often the pairs are assigned due to schedule availability, not teacher choice. Tennis doubles partners, pair ice skaters, and other close-knit teams are built through mutual selection, not who is available during third period.
- Teaching pairs need time to gel as a team. Most teachers work alone; being a teammate is a skill developed over years. Often, however, special education co-teachers work with two or even four different teachers a year, with new teammates each year.
- Common planning time is key. How can two teachers work as a team if they seldom plan lessons together. Very few co-teachers are afforded the opportunity to plan daily lessons with their partner.
- Mutual respect is the foundation of any partnership. At the secondary level, where content knowledge is prized by general education classroom teachers, a special educator's lack of deep content expertise can undermine trust.

When these elements are present, co-teaching can be very effective.

class or independent work.[4] This means that the second teacher was providing extra targeted help to struggling students just 13 percent of the period. That equates to six minutes of extra help a day. Is it realistic that a student can make up two years of skill gaps and misunderstandings in six minutes per day?

All kids who struggle benefit from extra time to learn, but this practice is least common, in my experience, in middle schools. It's not that sixth, seventh, and eighth graders need it less; in fact, it's crucial that students enter high school with a solid academic foundation. For many students, failing a single course in ninth grade can be a direct route to dropping out before graduation.

The obstacle is that for some, the middle school model, mindset, and schedule can undermine extra time for struggling students. Many of the middle schools I have worked with have strongly embraced more traditional forms of support, especially co-teaching or push-in, and resisted extra instructional time. Middle school principals and teachers have shared the following:

- The push-in/co-teacher can be more easily integrated into the middle school team model. For example, a special educator can be the sixth-grade co-teacher and attend all team meetings. A dedicated extra-time team might have to support students across multiple teams.
- Extra time differentiates student schedules based on differing student needs. Some middle schools want to avoid labeling or separating students, so no one feels different by being identified as needing extra help.
- Some kids missing an elective or foreign language to get extra math, English, or reading seems to matter more in some middle schools.

While these concerns are very legitimate, the historic practices haven't helped kids catch up and prepare them for success in high school.

In a case of unintended consequences, some middle schools have tried to merge their model with the best practices but come up short. One Midwestern middle school principal called me, quite excited. She had thought long and hard about the recommendation for extra time for struggling learners. After much soul searching and many faculty meetings, the school was moving forward with extra instructional time. The plan was that all sixth graders would get two periods of English.

I was stunned. Instead of praise, I blurted out a series of questions:

- What about math or reading?
- What about the seventh and eighth graders?
- Why have extra English for kids already doing just fine in English?

A bit crestfallen, she responded, "We can't do extra math and English. There is no time in the day for two extra periods. We felt it important not to segregate kids, so everyone gets the 'extra' time. The seventh- and eighth-grade staff wouldn't go along with shortening math, science, and social studies to give to English. You see, the sixth-grade team agreed to move to eight periods from seven to provide the extra time for double English."

Sadly, this didn't come close to actually implementing the best practices. To be sure, many middle schools have and can preserve what they value and shift toward what's more impactful for struggling students. I hope more will in the future. I just caution that some middle schools might need more time to plan and get comfortable with the six shifts.

WISDOM FROM THE FRONT LINES

Nothing can sum up the value of extra instructional time better than a group of teachers who actually do this important work. I asked a few such secondary teachers, "How it is going?" "Well" one said. "There is just so much to do. After assessing each student's needs, I made a plan to fill individual learning gaps, and I try to leave fifteen to twenty minutes a day for preteaching and reteaching current material. I see the list of skill gaps shortening, but there is so much to do and so little time to do it. We just have one period a day."

Just one period a day, she lamented. That is about 150 hours of instruction a year, 150 more hours than co-teachers, push-in teachers, and core teachers get. If she felt pressured with just 150 hours of teaching time to remediate, how must other teachers feel who don't get even fifteen minutes a year to cover prior material, reteach, or preteach as they race through this year's curriculum.

The six shifts that will reimagine special education, RTI/MTSS, and other supports for struggling students in a new era are all part of an interconnected system. Alone, none are a silver bullet. Together, they are a potent package. Core instruction is foundational, but not enough.

Extra instructional time targeted to students' specific needs is also re-quired. In addition to these first two shifts, who delivers the core in-struction and the extra instruction is a central component to raising achievement. Not just anyone can be the adult providing the instruc-tion. The following chapter explains why.

CHAPTER 4

Shift #3: From
Generalists to Specialists

THE PREVIOUS TWO CHAPTERS make the case that core instruction plus
extra time to learn are a powerful combination to help students
who struggle catch up and excel. There is, however, a missing ingredi-
ent to this formula for student success. *Who* provides the core instruction and the extra help matters as much as having 100 percent of core
and daily extra time.

The most obvious, most controversial shift is from generalists to
specialists. The implications of a simple, uncontroversial fact can cause
a lot of soul searching. Why does this statement trigger so much anxiety and reflection? "Teachers matter, a lot. For students who struggle,
they matter even more so."

In most districts that close the achievement gap, classroom teachers
are skilled at teaching a wide range of learners, and the staff providing
extra help in remediation and intervention or special education services
have depth and strengths in the content they are teaching. Teaching a
student who is two or more years behind is hard. This requires a skilled
teacher.

Looking back at history, it's hard to decipher why we used to think
that struggling students really benefited from generalists. Let's define
this term, since it's not in common use, even if we have more than half
a million of them working in schools today. A generalist is a teacher
who is asked to do it all. Teach reading, math, writing; manage behaviors; write IEPs; know the law; ensure compliance, and so on. Special

educators, for example, are generalists, despite having *special* in their title. Very few are given the opportunity to specialize in any one subject, skill, or function. A true specialist is a person with deep training, expertise, aptitude, and ability in a particular area, such as teaching reading, assessing for IEP eligibility, or managing behaviors.

Achievement-gap-closing districts assign content-strong teachers, the best they have, to support struggling students. They also allow others, like special educators and school psychologists, to play to their strengths. These other staff members are very talented, but no one is good at everything.

The obvious part of the shift to using highly skilled teachers is that the impact of great teachers on student achievement is well known and well documented. Most of us can remember that remarkable teacher who made chemistry, writing, or algebra finally make sense, perhaps even spurring a lifelong passion. The research couldn't be stronger. John Hattie's exhaustive twenty-year study of 1,200 meta-analyses concluded that teacher quality was the most impactful school-based variable driving student outcomes. Most educators quickly embrace this research, often accompanied by vigorous head nodding. Few question his research findings.

While obvious and significant, this finding is not always acted upon, especially with regard to teaching students who struggle. Based on my review of more than a hundred school districts, it seems the more students struggle, the further they get from highly skilled teachers who have training in the subjects being taught. An open-eyed look at how most schools serve students with mild to moderate disabilities, reading challenges, or other academic challenges reveals that most districts don't put this wisdom into actual practice. They act as if the exact opposite were true.

A medical analogy helps highlight just how odd common practice is in many schools. When going to a doctor, we expect that they are highly skilled and well trained in their field. If, during the examination, they find an irregular heart condition, they refer you to a cardiac specialist. Someone even more experienced, even better trained, and specializing in heart conditions will be asked to treat a patient with a serious need. If the diagnosis is severe, someone top in their field, with a proven track record in helping patients with similar needs, might be sought out. Clearly, these actions reflect that the quality of the doctor matters, as does specialized expertise. Very few in this situation would tolerate a doctor who had limited training in basic medicine; even fewer would agree to a referral to a nurse or nurse practitioner in the case of a worrisome heart condition, and none with a serious diagnosis would seek out the doctor's receptionist for advice and treatment.

Many schools, however, follow a path more analogous to the nurse practitioner, not the cardiac specialist, by turning to ever less skilled or less specialized help as the situation gets more serious. Yes, this is an overstatement, to make a point, but it's not a complete mischaracterization. The reality varies from classroom to classroom and school to school, but too often, the more children struggle, the further they get from a highly skilled teacher. First, a special educator, who may or may not have expertise in the content, is asked to help, and if the need is very great, a noncertified paraprofessional will be the desired source of support.

CONTENT-STRONG TEACHERS MAKE A BIG DIFFERENCE

The power of a content-strong teacher becomes evident when contrasted to the more typical generalist, a Jack or Jill of all trades. Most special educators are generalists, by design. The typical special education teacher is expected to teach an extra-help class or pullout session, often called resource room or academic support class. Even the name suggests that the help is content neutral, both the class and the teacher.

In a typical middle or high school resource room, five to ten students with various needs, IEP goals, and skill gaps go to a classroom staffed with a special educator and perhaps a paraprofessional, too. The teacher can't do a whole class lesson because the whole class doesn't have a common focus or need. A few students struggle with writing, some with geometry, others algebra, and perhaps some with reading comprehension. Rather than direct instruction, homework help or preparing for an upcoming test is the most common form of support. This support is generalized, because the diverse needs of the class prohibit specializing in one particular need or another.

After observing many resource rooms, I'm surprised by how often the teacher must thumb through the student's textbook for a quick refresher on how to answer a question the student asked. There are just too many subjects for any teacher to stay on top of them all. The teacher can't be specialists in all subjects because that's not what specialists do.

Now, consider a teacher who is strong in the content—a specialist—asked to work with a group of students all struggling in one subject, math, for example. Rather than needing a quick reminder on the formula for finding the area of a trapezoid or the derivative of a quadratic equation, a content-strong teacher can look at a student's incorrect answer and deduce that they multiplied rather than divided by two in the second step. The teacher can pinpoint misunderstandings based on the wrong answer and thus target instruction to this skill. The teacher will unteach the wrong method, then reteach the correct skills. Because many in the class may have the same challenge, this can be a whole-class mini lesson.

The other powerful tool in the content-strong teacher's arsenal is the ability to teach one idea multiple ways. By definition, students who struggle were taught a concept by their classroom teacher and yet didn't master it. Teaching it again the same way can be like speaking louder to someone who doesn't speak the language. Presenting the material in a different way can create that "Aha, now I get it" moment struggling students so greatly want and need.

Teaching multiple paths to understanding applies to both basic and complex ideas. I saw it in an exceptional elementary classroom applied to a very foundational skill.

The classroom teacher asked the class, "How much is 5 + 7?"

An eager girl raised her hand and correctly responded "12."

The teaching could have stopped there. All the kids who had the wrong answer on their homework could have scribbled the right answer next to their incorrect one. Instead, the teacher knew the value of multiple methods of teaching because she knew that kids learn the same concept in different ways. The teacher asked, "Sally, how do you get this answer?"

"Well, I know that 5 + 5 = 10 and I had two left over, so 10 +2 = 12," she proudly responded.

The teacher didn't stop and move on to the next question, however. She asked if anyone had a different way to get the right answer. Now, I was puzzled. As a former practicing engineer and general all-around math guy, I didn't know any other way to solve the equation. I always add numbers by getting close to the nearest multiple of 10 and add the remainder when doing simple addition.

Jose raised his hand and shared, "5 + 10 = 15 and because I went 3 too far, I walked back to 12." With a bit more prompting, Jose also shared with the class that he just remembered 5 + 7 = 12 and didn't really have a method.

In a few minutes, three different ways to add single-digit numbers were presented. For struggling students, it might take three or even four different approaches before one clicks. Content-strong teachers are much more likely to have multiple ways of teaching a single skill, which can move a student from confusion to clarity. It asks a lot to expect a generalist to have multiple ways of teaching math, vocabulary, comprehension, science, social studies, and so on.

In Minnesota, Wayzata High School, in a district of 10,400 students, embraced the first three shifts fully and faithfully. While a typical student in the district made two to three points of growth each year measured by MAP, the progress monitoring tool from NWEA, students in their double-time program with a content-strong teacher had 8.1 points of growth in the first year of the program. As teachers refined their skills, growth increased to nearly 11 points. That's more than three year's growth in a single year. While only 20 percent of students in the program started at grade level, 56 percent reached grade-level mastery at the end of year one, and 67 percent of students the next year.

SKILLS, NOT JUST CERTIFICATION

In all this discussion of skilled teachers and content-strong instructors, one word I haven't mentioned is *certification*. The law says teachers must be appropriately certified, but that's insufficient. Certification doesn't indicate what skills, strengths, and aptitude teachers have.

All special educators, for example, are certified to teach special education students, but some are strong teachers of reading, others are strong at math, and some are strong in behavior management, but not academics. Even elementary classroom certification isn't a great predictor of specialized content-strong expertise. Many certified classroom teachers lack training in teaching struggling students to read, for example.

Struggling students need teachers with both proper certification (because it's the law) and the required background and skills (because that's how they will master grade-level material). Teacher ability, training, and content expertise, not certification, should be the driving force for hiring and assigning teachers to help struggling students.

The most extreme example of not valuing, in practice, the importance of content-strong teachers with specialized skills is the widespread use of paraprofessionals to support students who struggle academically. In nearly all school districts across the country, I see students who struggle with assigned paraprofessionals. Most paraprofessionals are great people who care deeply, work hard, and bring passion to school every day, despite low pay. Despite all this heart, most paraprofessionals are not highly skilled, content-strong teachers. Few are teachers at all. Contrary to the ever-increasing evidence on the impact of teacher ability on student learning, the number of paraprofessionals keeps growing in the United States, even as student enrollment dips. The number of special education paraprofessionals has increased by 22 percent for the last ten years that we have data, while student enrollment inched up just 2.6 percent.[1]

Paraprofessionals do play a very important role in schools and for children with disabilities. They help manage behavior, assist students with health and safety concerns, are instrumental in supporting students with severe special needs like intellectual disability, facilitate inclusion, and can be valued extra helpers in kindergarten and preK classrooms.

These roles are important but overstated. Too often, principals and district leaders who value the importance of high-quality teaching are certain that the paraprofessionals in their school or district do the right things. I hear many say, "Our paras support behavior, health, and safety and aren't teaching struggling students." In fact, the more paraprofessionals a school has, the more certain people seem to be they aren't acting as teachers.

If you're thinking the same—"not in my school or district"—ask yourself how can you be sure? In thousands of interviews with paraprofessionals across the country, the majority share that they are instrumental in helping struggling students learn to read or do math. More than a few describe themselves as their students' "other teacher," and quite a few special educators use the same language. But ultimately, the only way to know for sure if paraprofessionals are acting as teachers is to collect detailed data.

In one suburban district with nearly twice as many paraprofessionals as similar districts and a stubborn achievement gap, the elementary principals held two convictions: (1) teachers matter, a lot, and (2) our paras only help with behavior, health, and safety. Interestingly, all the principals thought they needed more paraprofessionals. This puzzled me because the district was in a quiet suburban area, so if they had so many paraprofessionals, why did they have so many more behavioral needs than other districts? I was also surprised that they could be certain, since paraprofessionals in the schools didn't have detailed schedules. They were assigned to rooms or students but did not have hour-by-hour expectations. Simply put, how could anyone know what they really did?

To solve the mystery, we asked the paraprofessionals to record, in ten-minute increments, what they were doing for a week. The analysis amazed the principals. Fully 74 percent of paraprofessional hours were devoted to academics, not behavior, health, and safety. Mostly they worked providing direct small-group or one-on-one reading support.

Whether by plan or mission creep, all across the country, paraprofessionals in far too many schools are substituting for teachers of struggling students. The further a student falls behind, the further they get from a highly skilled teacher. In the hundreds of districts I have advised, elementary school students with mild to moderate special needs who struggle to read are more likely to get intervention from paraprofessionals than certified teachers. Students without disabilities who struggle to read may or may not get help from a skilled reading teacher, but their odds of getting intervention from a true reading specialist are many times better than a student with a disability.

BETTER ISN'T THE SAME AS GOOD

For schools and districts that undertake efforts to limit the role of paraprofessionals providing academic support, it can be a case of out of the frying pan, into the fire. The most common shift in this direction is from paraprofessionals to special education teachers, from noncertified to certified staff. All good, right? Maybe yes, but maybe no.

Having special education certification doesn't indicate that the teacher knows a lot of math or a little or if they are well trained in teaching reading or not at all. In many hundreds of interviews with special educators, hardworking, committed staff have shared, especially at the secondary level, that they are teaching subjects like algebra, physics, and others for which they have no formal training. In more than a few cases, these teachers shared that they struggled with these subjects in high school and avoided them completely in college. They teach these skills and subjects because we ask them to, but should we have asked in the first place?

Not just secondary special educators are asked to teach outside their areas of specialized training. At the elementary level, roughly two-thirds of special education teachers have no formal training in teaching reading, according to the 2015 National Council on Teacher Quality "Teacher Prep Ratings"; based on schedule-sharing data from tens of thousands of them, it's their primary activity day in and day out.[2]

Special educators, like all people, have areas of strength, and like all of us, few are expert at everything. This is equally true for academics and social and emotional support (see the sidebar "Expertise in SEB"). Unfortunately No Child Left Behind, Every Student Succeeds Act, and most school systems act as if special education teachers are masters of the universe—great reading teachers, strong at math, expert at identifying disabilities, skilled at a wide range of assessments, well trained in managing problematic behavior, up to date on the law, deft with parents, agreeable co-teachers, and so much more. No one person can do well all that we ask special educators to do every day. It is no wonder that all fifty states are experiencing a shortage of special education teachers, that they are leaving the profession faster than other roles, and that fewer are opting to enter the field. We have asked them to do too much, but because they care, they do it, until they burn out and leave the profession. Students and teachers alike deserve that we allow special educators to play to their strengths.

Staff morale and student learning rise when folks skilled in teaching reading teach kids who struggle to read; those strong in behavior help forestall outbursts; and those who relish the IEP process assess, write IEPs, and keep the district in compliance.

Allowing special educators to play to their strengths seems a simple, yet radical idea. General educators have been afforded this privilege for decades. No English teacher would be asked (or agree) to teach Algebra II, and biology teachers don't teach physics, even if they are in the same department. Hell, many geometry teachers don't want to teach algebra and vice versa, even though they are certified to teach both math classes.

In many schools, a single special educator at the secondary level teaches three or more subjects a day. No other teacher does or would. How many other staff are asked to teach across disciplines like math, English, and science?

The appeal of letting special educators specialize loses its shine once leaders start to think through the implementation. That thinking is not quick and easy, but it's worth the effort. Figure 4.1 summarizes one way of allowing staff to play to their strengths.

EXPERTISE IN SEB

Don't make a hard job even harder. Helping students with mental health needs, dealing with trauma, or mitigating behavioral challenges isn't easy, even for the best trained staff. It's complex and emotionally taxing. Some districts, however, regularly ask staff to provide services that the kids need, but that the adults aren't fully trained to provide. They say, "Will do," because they care, but in time burn out. The students don't benefit from their heroic actions either.

As I crisscross the country, I see people in a wide range of roles helping out with social, emotional, and behavioral (SEB) services. Nine roles to be exact: assistant principal, guidance counselor, school adjustment counselor, school psychologist, special educator, paraprofessional, social worker, mental health professional, and community partner. I suspect this list looks familiar and seems reasonable. But is it reasonable? Reorganizing the list by the amount of formal training folks have in mental health or behavioral management can be insightful.

No formal training
- Assistant principal
- Guidance counselor
- Paraprofessional

Many have formal training; many do not
- Special educator
- School psychologist

Extensive formal training
- School adjustment counselor
- Social worker
- Mental health professional
- Outside partner

What's most striking about the list is that many districts rely most heavily on the folks who lack formal training and have the fewest people with extensive formal training. Equally problematic is that the districts assume everyone in the middle group does have the requisite background skills, even though some do and some don't.

Every one of these roles brings needed skills to their schools, but they have different skills, such as:

- Managing the IEP process
- General counseling (trauma, depression, anxiety, etc.)

- Substance abuse counseling
- Behavior management, prevention, and coping skills
- Building relationships
- College and course planning

The key is to know your staff and their strengths and backgrounds and match them appropriately to the students' many needs. Titles aren't enough. A person-by-person assessment will serve students and staff well.

FIGURE 4.1
Sample areas of teacher strength

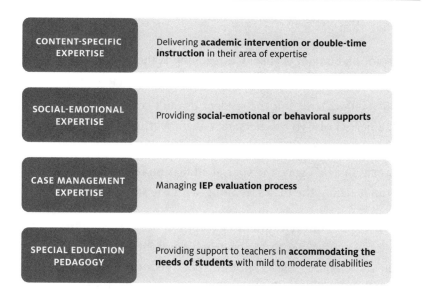

CONTENT-SPECIFIC EXPERTISE	Delivering **academic intervention or double-time instruction** in their area of expertise
SOCIAL-EMOTIONAL EXPERTISE	Providing **social-emotional or behavioral supports**
CASE MANAGEMENT EXPERTISE	Managing **IEP evaluation process**
SPECIAL EDUCATION PEDAGOGY	Providing support to teachers in **accommodating the needs of students** with mild to moderate disabilities

NOT AN EASY CONVERSATION

Some worry that it would be hard or insulting to identify teacher interest, aptitude, and skills. It's not. All you have to do is ask. In session after session with special educators, I have asked them to self-identify their strengths, and as long as their boss wasn't in the room, they readily shared their answer. When asked if they could focus mostly on X and hardly ever have to do Y, big smiles filled the room. Despite clear preferences and strengths, these teachers will come to work the next day and do X, and Y, and A, B, C, D, E, F, and G, too. Still, having a discussion of teacher strengths can be uncomfortable because it implies some people are better at X than others. Leaders shouldn't be afraid to raise the subject in a judgment-free way. No one can be great at dozens of unrelated tasks, topics, and content areas. Common sense, not courage, is needed.

Oddly, the only time I find school and district leaders comfortable acknowledging that not all special educators, for example, are equally strong across all domains of their work is when it comes to supporting co-teaching at the secondary level. A typical exchange sometimes goes like this:

SCHOOL OR DISTRICT LEADER: Co-teaching is the best of both worlds. We get general education and special education at the same time.

CONTRARIAN: True, but the student doesn't get extra time to learn. One period of two teachers isn't as impactful as two periods of one teacher, yet the cost is the same.

LEADER: But this way, the special education teacher is in the classroom learning the material along with the students.

I wish this conversation was rare, but it happens fairly often. A commonly stated reason for co-teaching is the open acknowledgment that at the secondary level, not all special educators are well versed in the content. Students who struggle need teachers who aren't just a few pages ahead in their own mastery. Certainly, many co-teachers are content strong, but too many are not, to the detriment if kids, teachers, and the budget.

The second hesitation in allowing special educators to focus is more practical: "What if we don't have enough people to focus on behavior, too few for math, and would anyone select the IEP assessment compliance role?" This fear of having the wrong mix of skills, interest, and aptitude is very legitimate. But consider the following: If you have the wrong mix, say, too many with compliance expertise and not enough with reading or math strength, isn't it better to know that you have staff doing work they don't like and don't feel well prepared to do. Not knowing is worse than knowing. Usually more than enough people seek out the IEP compliance assessment role, so there's no need to worry about this.

Like everything in the complex world of K–12, specialization shouldn't be taken to extremes. Might a person focusing on behavior also case-manage some IEPs or a reading-focused person also do a few math groups? Probably. Playing to strengths is a goal to work toward, rather than a hard and fast boundary.

If not enough special educators have the desired specialization, and they can't be expected to gain content expertise from general education peers, then how does a district get enough content-strong teachers to supplement its existing teaching staff? The largest pool of strong math teachers, English teachers, and reading teachers is general education. Many of the districts that have made dramatic gains in student achievement intentionally blur the lines between struggling students with and without special needs. This blurring works in both directions. Since kids with and without disabilities who have similar needs should get similar services, who provides services to these students should also be similar. General education and content strong, playing to their strength, special educators should each help struggling students regardless of their disability status.

At this moment, a special education director might be tempted to scream, "This is illegal. Only special educators can help kids with IEPs." A thoughtful review of the goals of IDEA's mandate for serving students in the least restrictive environment (LRE) says otherwise. In every state, the law says that kids with disabilities should be educated in the LRE. This means we should provide reading or math intervention or extra help by a general education teacher first, because this is the LRE. It's not just legal by a technicality; it meets both the spirit and letter of the law.

"But the IEP calls for resource room with a special education teacher, so we have no choice" is a commonly raised objection as well. This concern is legitimate, but easily remedied. Change, with the parent's participation and consent, the IEP, which should facilitate best practice and access to content-strong teachers, not prevent it.

The final worry about having general education specialists serve students with disabilities is financial. In some states, the state reimburses for the services special educators provide, but not if general education teachers provide the services. Fortunately, many states are moving away from this, but for those who might lose reimbursement, there are two considerations. First, kids deserve the best possible instruction, even if it costs more, and second, with slightly larger group sizes, even with less reimbursement, this approach might not cost much more than the less effective, but better funded alternative.

A less paradigm-shifting source of highly skilled teachers is to recruit them, rather than posting for and hiring generalists and hoping they have the needed skills, interest, and aptitude. When districts are short on staff with a particular needed area of specialization, they can fill these skill gaps through attrition. Over the course of a few years, as staff leave, the now available full-time equivalent can be filled by people who have the missing interest, aptitude, and training. Hiring becomes easier when the positions are posted with a stated area of specialization. In a competitive marketplace for new staff, advertising that special educators get to play to their strengths in your district can be a powerful draw.

The most difficult, but perhaps most commonly tried, strategy to grow the ranks of content-strong specialized teachers is professional development (PD) for current staff. A teacher who is strong in math or teaching reading can certainly benefit from related PD to become an even better teacher. But a teacher with little prior training, interest, or aptitude is unlikely to become a highly skilled math or reading teacher by attending a few workshops.

Most highly effective content-strong math teachers, for example, engaged and excelled in math in high school, studied math for four years in college, and then got a master's degree in how to teach math. It's hard to make up for a decade of training and lifelong passion in a few PD sessions or even a whole week of training in the summer.

One PD idea that just won't work but is also tried too often is attempting to create content-strong, highly skilled paraprofessionals. Teaching struggling students is hard and requires a highly skilled teacher. Few paraprofessionals will surpass the skills of a great teacher, except for the handful of dedicated souls who become paraprofessionals after being great teachers first.

NOT EASY, BUT WORTH THE EFFORT

Allowing staff to play to their strengths has many benefits, but one unintended, often undesired consequence. The long-held practice of assigning special education and intervention staff to a single school becomes more difficult.

Most teachers prefer working in just one school. The reasons are many: no wasted travel time, a sense of belonging, friendships with colleagues, and knowledge of the kids and the school culture. This preference is reasonable and helps explain, in part, why special educators and interventionists are so often asked to do so much.

What is the correlation between these two points? In small schools, there might be the need for just one or two special educators and one RTI interventionist. There is no need for a full-time person specializing in behavior or math or case management. These specialized roles might be just part of a full-time equivalent in each school. Fully utilizing their specialized skills requires one full-time equivalent split across two schools rather than a generalist in one school.

When sharing specialized staff across schools, districts can make efforts to honor and help shared staff so that quality of work life doesn't suffer. This includes:

- Allow staff to have a "main" school and "other" school. Their office and professional social life can be based at the main school.
- Expect shared staff to attend schoolwide meetings only at their main school, so they don't have twice as many meetings as their single-school colleagues.

- Coordinate the master building schedules of both schools to have similar bell schedules and rotation of the periods each day so their own schedules don't get overly complex.
- Help shared staff build their own schedules to minimize travel during the day. They could start at one school and switch schools at lunch, for example This usually requires a high level of coordination between schools and schedule-building skills.

Allowing staff to play to their strengths has other implications for staff assignments. Many elementary and middle schools assign special educators and interventionists to one or a few grade levels. "I work with first and second grade" or "I'm the seventh-grade special educator" is a common form of introduction. Again, this has all the same advantages of the elementary teacher being in a single school, but all the same disadvantages as well.

IMPROVING TEACHING OF CORE INSTRUCTION

The need for skilled and talented teachers applies equally to core instruction and intervention. Nearly all students spend most of their day in the general education classroom with a gen ed teacher, which is great. Ever since the passage of the No Child Left Behind Act, virtually all classroom teachers are certified and degreed. In some states, they are even required to have a master's degree. Despite their certifications, their college training, and even years of teaching experience, many classroom teachers report being underprepared to teach students with mild to moderate disabilities, students who struggle to read, or kiddos with other academic needs.

In over a thousand interviews with classroom teachers, I constantly hear general education staff share that they are uncertain how to meet the needs of their struggling students. It's not their fault. This isn't about finger-pointing, but rather pointing to a better way forward. In many schools, in order to implement a strategy of struggling students being well served by content-strong teachers with the skills needed to reach those students, classroom teachers need some help from the district.

Many teachers never learned how to teach struggling students. They were trained in an era when such kids went down the hall to other teachers and paraprofessionals. A study by the National Council on Teacher Quality reviewed course offerings and syllabi from nearly every teacher preparation program in the country; it found that only 37 percent of elementary and special education teacher prep programs is explicitly teaching how to teach reading in accordance with published best practices such as the What Works Clearinghouse or the National Reading Panel.[3]

The reason many classroom teachers feel ill prepared to help some students is that their teacher preparation programs didn't actually prepare them. This puts the onus on school districts to fill the gap in developing needed teacher skills, and some do. Many elementary schools have provided PD on teaching literacy, which is great. Sometimes, however, the PD focuses on implementing a purchased literacy curriculum, which is not the same as building a foundational understanding of how kids learn to read. Reviewing pacing guides, sharing published lesson plans, or handing out assessment schedules is not the same as training in the importance of phonics, how to explicitly teach comprehension strategies, and the tenets of best practices for reading.

Just as certification is necessary, but insufficient, good curriculum is necessary but also insufficient. Groundbreaking research by Harvard professor Thomas Kane showed conclusively that giving teachers great curriculum didn't raise achievement.[4] They also needed to build and change their teaching practices as well.

If we accept that teachers matter, and that many are underprepared to fully help their struggling students, then it's fair to ask, "What do we do about this?" How can schools build the capacity of classroom teachers to meet most of the academic needs of most of their students, including students with mild to moderate special needs? Here are three practical suggestions:

- Implement at scale high-impact instructional coaching
- Send teachers back to school
- Hire and assign classroom teachers differently

A skilled instructional coach can be the best investment in teachers' and kids' futures. Bruce Joyce and Beverly Showers' groundbreaking research and many subsequent confirmations of their work have reported big gains in teacher skill and student achievement through high-quality instructional coaching.[5] These results are in stark contrast to the more popular alternative of "sit and git" PD, where a presenter lectures to a bored group of teachers listening in their seats A wise and engaging PD presenter can impart good ideas and even inspire, but teachers seldom change practice when they go back in the classroom and close the door. A coach in the classroom, observing, modeling, and giving honest feedback can fill in the knowledge gaps that teachers didn't learn in school.

One way to understand the oversized impact of coaching is to consider how adults learn other complex skills, such as learning to be a great skier. Few trudge to a classroom, sit at a desk, and listen to a talented ski instructor lecture on how to ski. Sure, there would be a PowerPoint detailing when to shift your weight as you turn, maybe even a video on how to tackle an icy mogul patch, and so on. The instructor could even tell an inspiring story about a person who overcame a fear of falling to become a championship skier, but this isn't how you learn to ski. You get on the slope with a talented instructor and receive immediate feedback as you ski down the slope. You practice under supervision, shifting your weight again and again, time after time. And when it comes to skiing an icy mogul patch, you are actually on an icy mogul patch, often watching the instructor tackle the difficult stretch first. Learning to teach struggling students is similar to, but harder than, learning to ski. In real time, feedback, practice, and modeling make all the difference.

The other reason high-quality, intensive coaching can be so effective in raising teacher capacity becomes clear when you run the numbers. Traditional PD might involve a few afternoon sessions and may be a full-day conference as well. This totals about ten to fifteen hours of training a year. That's not a lot of time to learn a hard-to-master skill. Let's run the numbers for delivering well-managed coaching.

First a few assumptions: One full-time coach can optimally support twenty teachers. She can spend four hours a day coaching teachers and one-and-a-half hours working with kids. During this kid time, she is providing direct tier-two or -three instruction. This helps her to stay in touch (and help a lot of kids in need). This leaves nearly ninety minutes a day for planning and a lunch period. Finally, let's assume the coach has a thoughtful schedule that allows her to spend some time helping teachers during common planning time, thus supporting more than one teacher at a time.

What do these figures add up to? Over sixty hours of coaching *per teacher* each year. Best of all, most of the help is one-on-one in their own classroom. This exceeds the National Staff Development Council recommendation that teachers need fifty hours to learn a new skill. And keep in mind that the ten to fifteen hours of traditional PD can reinforce the coaching lessons.

MAKING COACHING EFFECTIVE

Some teachers and principals aren't big fans of instructional coaching. Some feel it is a luxury, and others have experienced instructional coaching with limited impact. Like every recommendation in this book, good ideas only get good results when they are implemented well. Too often, coaching isn't well implemented, and the results are disappointing. Effective instructional coaches should:

- *Be effective teachers themselves.* They are not learning on the job; the position is not being assigned as a thank-you to a soon-to-be retiring teacher. And the strategy is not to get the weakest teachers out of the classroom. Sadly, sometimes these are the selection criteria; thus, it is no surprise that some folks sour on the idea.

- *Have high emotional intelligence (EQ).* Working with teachers is different than working with kids.
- *Be comfortable giving honest feedback, but in a way that encourages rather than offends.*
- *Work with most teachers, not just the eager beavers, rising stars, or the most struggling teachers.* The greatest gains will come from teachers in the middle range of effectiveness.
- *Spend about four-and-a-half hours a day in classrooms with teachers, rather than spend much of the day planning, writing feedback, or creating documents.* Ski instructors spend most of their time on the slopes because that is where the learning happens.
- *Provide some direct intervention to struggling students in order to stay grounded in the realities of the life of a teacher.*

Whether instructional coaches should also be interventionists is a complex question. In my experience, it can help the coaches be better coaches. Soon after leaving the classroom, a coach can get a bit out of touch. One district, for example, appointed three superstar teachers as reading coaches. They had the full package, including IQ, EQ, drive, passion, and the respect of their colleges. One summer, they helped revise the reading assessment plan and rolled it out just before school started. They provided great PD and modeled how best to assess students to maximize teacher insights and pinpoint student needs. This all looked good.

By the end of the first week, however, the coaches had eaten their own cooking and it didn't taste very good. They realized that the full battery of assessment took up to 120 minutes per student (way too long) and some assessments yielded little actiona ble information, especially for high-performing students. Within a week, the coaches helped revise the assessment schedule. In other districts where coaches lead and guide but don't also work with kids, I've seen well-crafted, but excessive testing, for example, continue for years, generating frustration, noncompliance, and lack of mutual respect.

ALTERNATIVES TO INSTRUCTIONAL COACHING

An investment in coaching is partly to make up for what teachers weren't taught in college or grad school. Some districts fill this gap by trying to recreate the desired college-level courses. One district, for example, partnered with a local university that came into the district and taught college credit courses after school. The schedule was tied to the school schedule, making continuing education much more convenient for teachers. Since many staff took the same courses together, it also built trust, common language, and social connections.

Another district replicated a university experience itself. It hand-picked staff to teach a thirty-two-hour course, gave homework and grades, and offered lane credits, salary increases tied to advanced course work, for successfully completing the course, even though it wasn't actually affiliated with a university. This was so popular and impactful, the district made the course a requirement for all new teachers and, ultimately, at the request of teachers themselves, made it a three-year, required sequence. This support helped the district move from eighteenth in its peer group of twenty to sixth over five years, as math scores skyrocketed.

Both coaching and college-level courses offered by a district are big but necessary efforts to ensure that all struggling students are taught by well-prepared, highly skilled staff. But wouldn't it be nice if all this training wasn't required?

This question was first posed to me in the most unlikely of locales, north of the Arctic Circle while on vacation in a remote lodge in Norway. What were the odds that the proprietor had been a teacher and principal before retiring to run a Nordic haven in the middle of nowhere? Over dinner, I shared with him a few approaches for developing teacher capacity and the value of high-impact coaching. (Yes, this is what I talk about while on vacation.) Rather than nodding appreciatively as a host should do, or lavishing praise on my thinking in exchange for a great review on TripAdvisor, he shot back, brusquely, "Why do schools, for example, hire elementary classroom teachers who aren't already highly skilled at teaching reading or struggling students?" I was speechless. Why did we?

As I reflected on how most districts hire teachers, I realized that they considered many factors, but underlying the hiring of many new teachers was the idea that because they have a degree and are certified, they are ready to teach, including teaching students who struggle. Other districts just assume that they will have to supplement these skills. Some schools hire differently, reducing the need to build capacity in their staff. For example:

- Some partner with nearby teacher prep colleges to shape the course offerings to provide more of the needed skills as part of the undergraduate or graduate experience.
- Others prioritize specific skills, such as how to teach reading, during the selection process. They require prospective teachers to actually teach a class, including a reading lesson, thus ensuring new staff already have more of the most essential skills.
- Some districts welcome a multitude of student teachers and assess their skills during the practicum and make early offers to those demonstrating the training to be successful with struggling learners.
- A few principals I've met hire teachers with a couple of years of experience in districts that have already provided the critical training.

A FEW POTHOLES TO AVOID

A lesson learned the hard way is that some school and district leaders mistakenly assume content strength in one area implies or ensures strength in an adjacent area. The most common case is teaching secondary reading. Despite concerted efforts in most elementary schools to teach reading, lots of middle and high school students struggle with comprehension, vocabulary, or fluency. Nationwide, 64 percent of eighth graders struggle (basic or below basic) with reading, and in some urban districts, closer to 90 percent need to improve their reading skills.[6] Like students struggling in any subject, they will benefit from highly skilled and trained teachers. Most English teachers, however, are well-trained teachers of writing, making sense of literature, and so on. They assume their students can read well but are not typically trained to teach them to read. Dedicated, skilled reading teachers are needed.

The other common hard-learned lesson is assuming that a strong teacher will be a strong instructional coach. While the inverse is never true, being an effective teacher is just part of the puzzle. Being able to work effectively with adults matters just as much.

Of all the lessons learned the hard way about providing struggling students more instruction from skilled content-strong staff, the road from paraprofessionals to skilled certified teachers is the path most littered with potholes. When districts commit to providing struggling students instruction by well-trained content-strong teachers, the transition can be a little rough. Kids will adapt and benefit instantly, but adult considerations often stymie the best of intentions. The biggest stumbling block is often shifting from paraprofessionals to teachers. This can be difficult for lots of reasons, such as:

- Paraprofessionals are community members and taxpayers.
- The schools may be the employer of choice for many hourly workers.
- Paraprofessionals are nice people and beloved by teachers and parents alike.
- Classroom teachers worry that the loss of an extra adult will mean more work for them.
- Parents fear less attention and support for their child.

These concerns are all legitimate and real, but fortunately they can be mitigated. The most common mistake I see (and have made myself) is assuming that the benefits of having great teachers will win the support of others for the shift in instructors. This seldom carries the day. Pushback against fewer paraprofessionals and more teachers quickly becomes intense.

Based on my guidance of more than fifty districts through this maze, I have found that a number of successful strategies have emerged:

- *Attrition is your friend.* No one should ever lose their job as part of the shift from paraprofessionals to teachers. As paraprofessionals leave of their own accord, replace them with certified staff.
- *Message the win, not the loss.* Don't describe the shift as a move to fewer paraprofessionals, but as more instruction from highly skilled and trained certified staff.
- *Provide written guarantees.* Parents rightfully wonder if a paraprofessional is removed from an IEP, a legally binding commitment dissolves in exchange for a promise of better services. A bird in the hand . . . Some districts provide written, signed assurances of general education supports for struggling students such as, "Any child scoring below benchmark will receive thirty minutes a day, five days a week of extra reading help from a certified teacher." This replaces one guarantee with a better one.
- *Never cut before you add.* Any reduction in paraprofessional support must come at the exact same moment that you add new certified staff; otherwise, a potential shortage will exist. For example, a budget vote adding X certified staff and reducing Y paraprofessionals through attrition pairs the addition and subtraction and ensures sufficient staff. Many teachers, principals, and parents fight the reduction of paraprofessionals because they fear that more skilled staff won't be hired in their stead.

- *Don't throw out the baby with the bath water.* The goal is never to reduce paraprofessionals; it's to provide the most appropriate and impactful supports for kids. Paraprofessionals play an important role in health, safety, and behavior. A matrix of student need is a powerful document for clarifying which supports are best suited for each situation. The matrix of student need is a district-developed guideline (not a hard and fast policy) that clarifies if a student has a particular need, then a particular support is most likely the best.

The key is to provide the best, most appropriate supports needed, and to foster lifelong independence—no more support than needed for no longer than needed. One district created a very structured process to determine when and how to deploy paraprofessionals. See the example in the appendix at the end of the chapter. Another district summarized its guidelines for matching paraprofessional support to student needs as indicated in table 4.1.

Providing struggling students instruction by skilled, content-strong teachers can seem obvious, desirable, and daunting, all at the same time. It's critically important, but not easy. I'm often asked why we can't give all kids 100 percent of core instruction and extra time to learn as well, and deal with the challenge of who provides this instruction later? Isn't two out of three shifts a big step in the right direction?

Unfortunately, the answer is no. This approach has contributed to the decades-long achievement gap. There is no workaround for high-quality, effective teaching; it requires staff that are appropriately trained and content strong. The first three shifts, as a set, are a powerful lever for raising achievement, but if any one of them is missing, it's no more useful than a two-legged stool.

TABLE 4.1

Matching support to best meet student needs

Type of Need	Nonparaprofessional help	"INDEPENDENCE IS THE LONG-TERM GOAL."	
		Paraprofessional support matrix	
		Shared and partial day/week paraprofessional support	Full-time or 1:1 paraprofessional support
Academic	• Reading teacher support • Accommodations by general education teacher • Additional general education support • Special education teacher instruction	• Not appropriate • If assigned, only for targeted subjects • Not during related services, resource room, etc.	• Not appropriate
Behavior	• Behaviorist support • Sensory diet	• Short-term intervention • Can be shared support	• Not appropriate
Social protection	• Peer support	• Only during lunch and recess	
Mobility	• Peer support	• Only between classes	
Health		• Can be shared in most cases	• Not appropriate
Resource room support	• Do not schedule more than 9 students		• Not appropriate
Substantially separate classroom support		• Reduce support when fewer students in the room (hour-by-hour schedule) • Assign to class, not student	

Paraprofessional management process

_____ School District

PROTOCOL, TOOLS, AND MANAGEMENT PROCESS
Elementary Level

Protocol

The _____ School District can use the following Student Abilities and Support Matrix as a tool to clarify students' needs and supports. It draws on the work Mueller and Murphy, Giangreco, and the District Management Group. Coupled with the guidelines for best practices, the CST process can ensure student academic success and lifelong independence. You will find the tool, as well as accompanying tips, on the following pages. These data inform the support strategy for that particular student.

Michael Giangreco, professor in the Department of Education at the University of Vermont and head of the Center on Disability and Community Inclusion, has some useful thoughts on the data that should inform the need for a paraprofessional.

Looking at student characteristics alone or too heavily puts a disproportionate emphasis on identifying what's wrong with the student without adequately considering whether characteristics of the school, classroom, personnel, or organization contribute to the perceived need for paraprofessional support. Similarly, decisions about paraprofessional support based on categorical labels (e.g., autism, deafness, multiple disabilities, etc.) are highly questionable given the heterogeneity of students labeled in any category and the wide variations of severity identified from school to school and person to person.

To give students "only as specialized as needed and only as much as needed" support, the district will ask adults who know the student and the school to complete the tool below. The data in this tool—as well as the tips that follow it—will help administrators and educators develop program, placement and support strategies that are designed to raise achievement and foster lifelong independence. Two notes on the process:

1. It is important that classroom staff who know the curriculum, activities, and the characteristics of the classroom complete as much of the tool as they can and then gather any necessary data from family and other administrators.
2. Complete the tool working column by column, from left to right.

Student's abilities and support matrix

	ABILITIES		SUPPORT	
	What the student can do without support	What the student cannot do without support	How could peers provide support and/or enable social acceptance?	How could certified staff support the academic or behavioral needs?
Arrival				
Classroom time (list subject and time of day)				
Classroom time (list subject and time of day)				
Classroom time (list subject and time of day)				
Classroom time (list subject and time of day)				
Recess				
Lunch				
Transitions/bathroom breaks				
Specials				
Departure				

Tips for completing the abilities/support matrix

1. **What can/can't the student do alone?**

   Does the student have personal and physical needs they can't satisfy on their own? For example:
   - Food
   - Medication or medical procedures, e.g., catheterization, respiration
   - Physical repositioning or posture
   - Restroom, diapers
   - Mobility, orientation
   - Dressing or equipment, e.g., leg braces
   - What supports do they received outside of school

   Does the student need to be prevented from harming him/herself or others? For example:
   - Wandering off or running away
   - Hurting self
   - Falling
   - Putting inedible items in mouth
   - Hurting others

   Does the student present behavioral issues that disrupt the education process for others?
   - Hitting
   - Self-stimulation
   - Resisting activity changes or directions
   - Taking others' things
   - Making violent choices

   Does the student suffer from attention deficit needs? For example:
   - Trouble staying on task
   - Not completing assignments
   - Can't sit still
   - Not focused

   Does the student present with social needs?
   - Job/skill development
   - Prompts to interact with peers
   - Social instruction
   - Protection from peers, other students, adults

2. Consider specifically *when and where* during the school day a student has particular gaps in their ability to manage on their own.

3. Consider in the best of all possible worlds, *who is best able* to provide the support needed by this student?

   Explore opportunities for *"natural supports"*—teachers, classmates, nurses, and others who would be present *even if the student with a disability was not in the classroom.* Could these natural supports:

   - Provide more instructional opportunities, e.g., preteaching, repeated practice?
   - Adapt instructional methods, curriculum, or materials?
   - Provide assistance with mobility?
   - Provide assistance with personal care?
   - Create a positive behavior support plan?
   - Create classroom and school-site accommodations?
   - Provide communications support?
   - Teach others about the student?
   - Ensure regular communication with the student's family?
   - Record class notes?
   - Facilitate small-group instruction?

4. Consider alternatives and adjustments to the physical characteristics of the school, classrooms, and grounds.

   These could involve:

   - Removing barriers
   - Using adaptive equipment or assistive technology
   - Rearranging furniture or other items in the student's environment
   - Controlling the physical climate, lighting, acoustics
   - Changing classroom student assignments and student characteristics
   - Changing classroom configurations and student's seating location
   - Creating a crisis management plan

5. Paraprofessional assignment sheet

   Once the student's abilities and supports matrix is complete, it should be shared with the CST/Central office to determine if, when, and how a paraprofessional is needed. If there is agreement that a paraprofessional is needed, that in turn should inform the creation of a paraprofessional assignment sheet (see below). *Note: a paraprofessional will very likely be assigned to more than one student.*

Note: The paraprofessional assignment sheet must be signed and dated by the principal and _____. The assignment sheet is meant to help paraprofessionals, their managers, and the central office monitor the deployment of paraprofessionals districtwide and within each school.

Paraprofessional assignment

TIME	STUDENTS(S)*	ROLE	TARGET DATE FOR REEVALUATION	WHO WILL DIRECT THE PARAPROFESSIONAL
Arrival/departure				
Class/Time				
Class/Time				
Class/Time				
Recess				
Lunch				
Transitions/ bathroom breaks				

Principal: _____ Central Office _____ Date: _____

*Please indicate which student, if any, is your primary responsibility if there are personal safety/health needs to be attended to.

Shift #4: From Deterrence to Prevention to Better Address Social, Emotional, and Behavioral (SEB) Needs

N O PLAN FOR IMPROVING outcomes for students who struggle can be complete without a deep look at how best to meet their social, emotional, and behavioral (SEB) needs. This chapter will discuss the question of what to do, and the next chapter, the vexing question of how to implement that strategy when resources are limited and teachers are stressed out.

Even if a teacher, school, or district fully implements the three interconnected shifts discussed in the prior chapters, that's not enough to raise achievement for all struggling students. Schools can't improve academic outcomes without also addressing students' SEB needs. Kids have little chance to learn math, reading, critical thinking, and more, when they are feeling insecure, overwhelmed, or stressed. If students' mental health needs aren't met, the students aren't ready to learn no matter how good the teaching or curriculum.

The shift to prevention-based SEB supports is tightly connected to the first three shifts. Remember, it's not academics *or* SEB; they are two sides of the same coin. The interconnections are many. If discipline leads to lost instructional time, struggling students miss core instruction and ultimately have less time to learn. Conversely, providing strong academic interventions like extra time to learn reduces student anxiety over academic failure and, in and of itself, reduces a common behavior trigger.

While SEB supports have always been important, they have moved to the forefront in recent years. First, the kids walking through the schoolhouse doors today have greater needs. A decade ago, most incidents of violent, disruptive behavior were in middle and high schools. Back then, referrals for behavior-related IEPs peaked in seventh to ninth grades. Today, we're just as likely to see four-, five-, or six-year-olds bringing a class or even a whole school to a standstill due to problematic behavior.

Not only are these challenges starting at earlier ages, but they are more prevalent as well. As demographics have shifted over time, the majority of students in public schools live in poverty and/or come from homes with great stress. Students living in poverty have moved to many suburban districts, bringing different home-life challenges that are new to the former mostly middle-class towns. Even in affluent communities, student stress and anxiety are rising. Students with depression, for example, is increasing. From 2009 to 2017, the number of middle and high school students reporting a major depressive episode increased more than 50 percent, encompassing more than one in every eight students. During this same time, adult depression held basically constant.[1] In short, more kids have more SEB needs at younger ages than ever before.

To further complicate an already complicated situation, our emerging understanding of race and unconscious bias is deeply entwined with how schools address SEB needs. Over 50 percent of students in public schools are minorities, while the overwhelming majority of teachers and administrators are not. This discrepancy has magnified the challenge and complicated efforts to address the need.

If these reasons alone aren't a strong enough call to action, then staff burnout should be a compelling reason to shift how districts address student SEB needs. As I crisscross the country sharing best practices for

SEB supports, I'm always saddened by the folks who approach me at the end of the session. One principal in Colorado spoke for so many:

> We need to do more, but it's too late for me. I'm retiring, four years earlier than I wanted to, but my husband says I haven't come home unstressed in the last two years. And he is right. I love my job and all my kids, but a few are out of control and I don't know what to do. My teachers are leaving too. I had a great second-year teacher walk away from the profession because I couldn't help her manage the behavior of a highflier in her class. She was worn out and disappointed and so am I. It's too hard, and nothing seems to help

She wasn't an isolated case. In surveys conducted by the District Management Group over the last few years of approximately four hundred principals and assistant principals across the country, fully 86 percent indicated that they had experienced an increase in the number of students with emotional or behavioral disabilities over the last five years, yet only 30 percent reported that their respective districts were providing sufficient support and services to meet the needs of these students.

BIG EFFORTS, LITTLE IMPACT

What's most remarkable about this all too common situation is that the Colorado principal's district had made a full-scale effort to address SEB needs. It had created a new PBIS (Positive Behavioral Intervention and Supports) department, hired a top-notch department head, added certified behavior specialists, increased the number of paraprofessionals, and flooded schools with PD. Yet despite this heroic effort, the net result was staff retirement, resignation, and stress.

This incongruity highlights the reality of the state of SEB efforts in many districts. In interviews in many dozens of districts across the country, I see a divide between the central office and classroom teachers.

District administrators proudly list the many new efforts they have rolled out in the last five years. With pride, they share such efforts as restorative justice, responsible classrooms, PBIS, behaviorists, behavior coaches, PD on de-escalation, culturally responsive classrooms, trauma-informed instruction, and so on. Yet, classroom teachers in these very same districts simply say, "Yup, we got lots of new staff and programs, but the problem persists and gets worse each year."

To effectively meet the SEB needs of students, districts must adopt a comprehensive approach to the growing need, grounded in a focus on prevention, rather than deterrence. They must also learn to implement well these hard-to-implement efforts.

Addressing the SEB needs of students isn't one challenge; it is six. (See figure 5.1.) I have never met a chief academic officer or superintendent who said, "This year we are focusing our efforts on improving academ-

FIGURE 5.1
The six domains of social, emotional, and behavioral support

ics." This overly broad statement seems nonsensical and unfocused. A much more likely goal statement might be, "We are working on revamping our early literacy approach or implementing a new phonics program or rethinking middle school math instruction." Yet, it's very common to hear that a district is focusing on SEB or social emotional learning. This extremely broad focus undermines the chance of success.

As I have helped districts across the country, I see the SEB work falling into six domains. Districts must address all six, but perhaps not all at the same time, including:

1. *Universal behavioral expectations and classroom routines.* These are established norms for students and teachers alike, common expectations for daily interactions, and the foundation for a welcoming and safe environment.

2. *Social emotional competencies such as grit, empathy, and cooperation.* Society and the modern workplace have added to what's required to be a good citizen, a decent person, and an effective employee. Reading, writing, and arithmetic haven't been enough since the dawn of the knowledge economy. Critical thinking and problem solving were added to the list two decades ago. More recently, as the world has become more diverse and changed more quickly, and the nature of work is more team based, a well-educated person needs social emotional skills as well.

3. *Mental health counseling, substance abuse support, and social work services.* These direct supports to students and their families help address the stresses and complexities of modern life. They help students get to a place where they are ready to learn. In some countries, agencies provide these services, but in the United States, K–12 schools fill the void.

4. *Building trusting relationships between students and adults.* Not all kids learn just because they should or we want them to. They learn when they are engaged in school and see the purpose of learning and, most importantly when someone who cares about them wants them to learn. They might not engage

deeply for their own benefit, but they will do it for a teacher who cares about them. Just as athletes push themselves so they don't disappoint their coach or personal trainer, kids rise to great heights for their trusted, caring teacher. The opposite is unfortunately also true. If they think no one cares, then why should they care.

5. *Discipline practices and policies for minor or moderate infractions.* Despite clear expectations and thoughtful norms, some kids cross the line and violate behavioral expectations. Reasonable consequences, interventions, and steps should be taken. Consistency and clarity should guide the response.

6. *Addressing severe behavioral challenges.* A few students, perhaps 2 to 3 percent in a typical school, exhibit significant, often violent, nearly always extremely stressful and disruptive outbursts. Helping these students is a special case, different from the prior five.

Prevention permeates all six domains. With established universal expectations, students will not accidentally break rules or norms they didn't know about. Uniform classroom routines help students prepare and function in class without inadvertently confusing what's okay with Mrs. Smith but not okay with Mr. Jones. Teaching empathy and collaboration gives kids the reason and tools to reduce bullying, and counseling helps address many causes of students acting out or tuning out. Building trusting relationships supercharges prevention because it gives students a reason to stay on the right side of the line; addressing the most severe behavioral needs by stopping them before they happen is the epitome of prevention.

Thinking about SEB as six domains instead of one helps in many ways. It ensures that you address all the needs, not just some. One district, committed to addressing SEB needs, worked with all teachers in the district to establish classroom norms, revised the discipline code, and embedded direct instruction for developing empathy into the curriculum. This is a lot, and they did it pretty well. The central office hung a mission accomplished banner (figuratively) at a school board meeting as they shared details of the successful rollout. The teachers responded with rage, not praise or thanks. There were no social workers or counselors in many of the schools, and problematic behaviors were increasing. The district did half of a good job but hadn't addressed all the domains.

Not planning for all the domains also leads to misapplying good ideas from other domains. The adage, if all you have is a hammer, everything starts to look like a nail, comes to mind when a district addresses only some SEB domains. One school, for example, had embraced restorative justice circles. This thoughtful, at times effective, practice of discussing the impact of inappropriate behavior enables the aggressor to better understand the consequences and make amends, for example. Since this was the primary focus of the district's SEB effort, teachers and principals used it widely. It worked well for playground bullying but came up short when a student pushed a teacher hard into a wall. A good approach for one domain (minor discipline infractions) misapplied (to severe behavioral supports) to another ceases to be a good approach.

Perhaps the greatest cost of the lack of specificity about which domain a district is addressing for each program or strategy is the negative impact on staff morale. When leaders aren't clear, teachers fill in the details. One district, in near revolt, is an example. A very wise and capable leader rolled out a smart and well-implemented set of classroom and school norms and routines. The training was solid, and the plan design was right on the mark. The administrator was very proud that she had helped create a tier-one, universal set of expectations and norms. Unfortunately, she didn't tell the district: "This year we are rolling out and supporting the creation of universal tier-one norms, which are foundation for addressing the remaining five domains." She did say, over and over, that the district was addressing social and emotional learning (SEL). Every time she made this claim, classroom teachers, who desperately wanted help with domain six issues—severe behaviors—assumed that's what the SEL rollout was intended to address.

They saw this tier-one effort as useless in dealing with their top concern, and their rage festered.

Here is a tip to improve morale. Never say SEB or SEL in public without quickly qualifying which domain you are referencing. Clarity helps target the effort, and staff won't misunderstand the intended outcome.

There is great power in thinking about the six domains as distinct, and there is also strength from seeing them as interconnected. The overarching theme of the six domains is a focus on prevention, rather than deterrence. Prevention means stopping something undesirable before it happens by first removing the trigger. Deterrence stops unwanted acts but relies on the threat of negative consequences to forestall the undesirable actions.

WHERE TO START?

Over time, every district needs a comprehensive, well-implemented plan for all six domains, but where should it start? I've listed the domains in logical order, starting with broad foundational strategies and then the efforts that have an impact on fewer students. Starting with universal expectations can seem sensible, but classroom teachers are begging their leaders to first address domain six, severe behaviors. Students, especially students of color, receive unfair treatment, and many schools desperately need to update their approach to discipline (domain five), so many students desperately need high-quality counseling and mental health services (domain four). While every district is different, the people on the front line often want to start at the end and work their way back to the beginning. In deference to the classroom teachers and students most underserved or unfairly served, let's look at each of the six domains in reverse order.

Domain 6. Addressing severe behavioral needs

Roughly 2 percent of students, a handful in every school, cause an overwhelming amount of teacher, principal, and peer anxiety. These students often exhibit explosive and sometimes violent outbursts, often directed toward others, and are always disruptive and upsetting. After nearly every talk I give on the subject, a teacher or principal approaches me to say they are retiring early or leaving the profession because of one or two students who are out of control but not out of the school or classroom.

In years past, when violent outbursts were mostly confined to middle and high schools and occurred at a rate of only a few kids in every thousand, out-of-district placements or alternative schools were the (less than excellent) answer. As the number of such out-of-control students has increased and are now commonplace at ages four, five, and six, the old strategy isn't right for today (and wasn't very good for kids then either).

A big part of what makes such students stressful for teachers is that while it's easy to learn who these students are, it's hard to know when they will "explode." In James Bond movies, all the bombs have easily viewed digital timers that give ample warning before the bang. Kids don't have countdown clocks on their foreheads. Even when a student seems to be having a good day . . . bang! . . . out of the blue, an explosive outburst can take place. Many teachers walk on eggshells and never fully relax because a student could erupt at any moment for no apparent reason.

Actually, not true! A more accurate statement is that to the teacher, the outburst *appears* to be out of the blue, but extensive research shows otherwise. Most students' problematic behaviors have *very specific* triggers, but these triggers are hard for untrained folks to see.

I experienced this firsthand and was initially very skeptical of this trigger concept. Early in my time as a superintendent, a flustered and exasperated principal approached me about a second-grade student. The principal said, "John [not his real name] has to go. He is violent and dangerous, and his teacher is on the verge of walking out. She's been to the union, and parents are dusting off their torches and pitchforks. We have all had enough." Even though John's classroom teacher had seven years' experience, a few as a special educator, she could not stop John hurling desks, chairs, and staplers regularly. She had been hit by a stapler that morning, the last straw.

As a new superintendent, I wanted happy principals and teachers, and I readily (not my finest hour) agreed to support an out-of-district placement for the student. I placed the safety of others (and my career) over, perhaps, the education and socialization of John. It felt like an either-or situation.

To my great disappointment, we couldn't find a school or program that had an opening for John. While we continued to frantically look for an out-of-district solution, we also sought a stopgap measure. With no expectation of success, I hired a behaviorist to come to the school for three days. To be fully honest, this was mostly a political move to show we were taking steps and doing something while we continued to look for a permanent solution.

After spending two full days with John, observing him in the classroom and in one-on-one discussions with both John and the teacher, the behavior specialist announced, "I know why John is acting out. It's the teacher." This seemed ridiculous and insulting. I was wondering if I could get my money back or at least not pay for the third day we had contracted for. The teacher was caring, experienced, and trying hard. She was exhausted, but always kind and professional.

"What was the teacher doing?" I asked, with a bit more sarcasm than intended. The answer was shocking. Before the last two "out of the blue" outbursts, the teacher had asked John: "How was your weekend?" "What was your answer to question #6 on the homework?"

This didn't make any sense to me. The teacher was just being a regular, everyday teacher, at least that's how it appeared to an outsider. The behaviorist explained how John had processed these questions. She shared his inner monologue. Here's how John experienced these interactions with the teacher: "She hates me! She always embarrasses me in front of my classmates. She doesn't want me to have friends!" His anger was building as he explained, even though nothing was further from the truth. He continued, "When she asked me how my weekend was, she *knew* my dad came home angry and the police were called. She *wanted* me to say this while Steve and Mike were close enough to hear so they would tease me and not be my friends or ever come to my house. So, I pushed her so she'd shut up."

In reacting to the second question, turning red, John retorted, "And the other time she embarrassed me again, got me so mad when she asked me that really hard question [#6 on the homework]. She knows I don't understand this stuff. She wanted me to look stupid in front of everyone [she didn't, of course], so I threw a stapler at her [to avoid having to answer the question]." What looked like good, everyday teaching to most felt like a full-on personal assault to John.

With this understanding in hand, the behaviorist spent the third day working out a plan with John and the teacher:

1. The teacher would ask John how he is doing when others aren't in earshot.
2. John and the teacher would communicate secretly. He would point a pencil away from him if he wasn't ready to answer a question.
3. When he felt the tension rising within, he would immediately, without asking permission, stand up and walk twice around the hallways while breathing deeply and slowly and then sit back down.

Three days of observation, discussion, probing, and planning (plus a pencil) avoided the need for a decade of outplacement. The last time I checked, John was in seventh grade and doing well in his neighborhood school.

Who knew that a good, caring teacher was inadvertently causing John's violent outbursts? The What Works Clearinghouse knew; so did Ross Greene, author of *Lost at School* and *The Explosive Child*, and Jessica Minahan and Nancy Rappaport, authors of *The Behavior Code*, to name just a few behavior gurus, know that triggers can appear like benign interactions. Behavior management is a science, and schools need folks with this expertise.

One New York City high school that served students with behavioral challenges seemed as if it was hoping against reason that it could dramatically reduce problematic behaviors without resorting to tough discipline. After much soul-searching and accepting that traditional measures weren't effective, the staff went on a journey for a better solution. After much discussion and preparation, they committed to building stronger, more authentic two-way relationships with their students and invest in prevention-based strategies to find and address triggers and manage behavior. Given the high level of staff buy-in nearly two years in the making, great things started to happen. Serous behavioral incidents dropped from 341 to 138 in just one year. Two years later, the number was just 66. Staff and students both noted how much safer and welcoming the school had become.

When prevention efforts aren't in place, the common alternative is to place students with problematic behaviors in special classrooms. With the best of intentions, caring staff try to help kids in need by referring them to special education. A helpful intervention for many, it is often a step back for students with problematic behavior. They need help for sure, but help that is prevention based and will find and eliminate the triggers. One small study reflects what I have seen across the country.

The Marshall Memo, a great digest of educational magazine articles, summarized the findings. In the memo, Eleanor Craft (Palm Beach County Public Schools) and Aimee Howley (Ohio University) reported on their study of nine African American students' experience in secondary-school special education classes.[2] On the positive side, students appreciated working with responsive teachers, getting more individual attention in smaller classes, and not feeling rushed. On the negative side, students felt stigmatized by peers, made limited academic progress because of the slow pace of the curriculum, and confronted barriers that kept them from returning to general education placements. Only a few of the students believed the benefits of special education outweighed the costs.

Craft and Howley found that these students' school behavior initially deteriorated because of traumatic events in their lives. Then their behavior problems and subsequent disruption inside and outside classrooms prompted teachers to refer them for special education services.

"Once they became eligible to be served via an IEP," say the authors, "the students found that their special education placement became a dead end, offering almost no chance for placement back in the general education program."

Domain 5. Discipline practices and policies for minor or moderate infractions

Discipline is the Achilles heel of prevention. Embracing prevention requires revising discipline practices to consider if a student can manage his or her behavior (yet) or not. Discipline must also support academic best practices and address inequitable application.

One obstacle to improving discipline is thinking the current case is okay: "We already focus on prevention. We have PBIS and other whole-school efforts" is a common refrain when school and district leaders first hear about a shift to prevention-friendly discipline.

By clearly setting expectations for proper behavior, social interactions, respect, and so on, and providing students with direct instruction on how to be good classroom citizens, schools are working to prevent problematic behavior. These clear expectations are typically coupled with discipline consequences for violating the norms. I call this "thoughtful deterrence." Tell kids what's expected, teach them how to do it, model it, and then have repercussions for not complying. This works for many, if not most, students.

I have a few questions for you:

- Did you ever get expelled while in school?
- Did you ever get mad at a teacher or classmate while in school?
- Did you ever want to say something ugly to a teacher or shove a classmate?

If you're like me, the answer to the first question is no, but yes to the other two. Thoughtful deterrence worked for us. We knew what was expected, feared the consequences, and thus controlled our desires. We didn't scream at our teacher or shove a classmate.

Today, just as when we were students, deterrence works for many (but not all) students. Unfortunately, a growing number of kids can't control their problematic behavior, even when they know and fear the consequences. For these students with the most problematic behaviors, prevention can't be primarily about deterrence, but rather mitigating triggers and building skill, because these kids don't know how to behave better. As Ross Greene, a leading behavior management specialist says, "They are behaving as well as they know how."

Let's not forget the points I made in previous chapters when considering what effective, just discipline looks like in the new era. Any plan that regularly reduces a student's access to instruction, except in the case of student or teacher safety, doesn't seem right. In fact, it likely fuels future lost learning time and more academic and behavioral challenges. The repercussions for acting improperly shouldn't be less learning. The use of in-house suspension paired with tutoring and working on real-time class assignments is more advantageous than sending kids home to play video games and fall academically further behind. And don't forget to assign content-strong teachers to the in-house suspension classes.

When short-term stints out of school are appropriate, rigorous online learning and regular electronic interactions with teachers can help reduce the academic consequences of suspension. If long-term removal to alternative schools is needed, make sure these schools also address student academic needs.[3]

Once discipline practices are redesigned to support teaching and learning best practices and consider students' ability to manage their actions, the practices must be applied equitably to all students. No shift to prevention can be fully effective without addressing unconscious bias in discipline.

Black students, boys, and students with disabilities were disproportionately disciplined (e.g., suspensions and expulsions) in K-12 public schools, according to GAO's analysis of Department of Education (Education) national civil rights data for school year 2013-14, the most recent available. These disparities were widespread and persisted regardless of the type of disciplinary action, level of school poverty, or type of public school attended. For example, Black students accounted for 15.5 percent of all public school students but represented about 39 percent of students suspended from school.[4]

This is disproportionate by 2.5 times.

Moreover, black students with disabilities lose three times as many instructional days due to discipline than their white peers. They lose, on average 12.1 days a year, roughly 2.5 weeks of core instruction.[5] Sadly, in some places, it's over 20 days per student.

Even before kindergarten, the problem is significant. Preschool children who were black made up 42 percent of all students who received one out-of-school suspension and 48 percent of those who received more than one such suspension, despite comprising just 18 percent of preschool enrollment.[6]

At this point, some readers might be thinking, yes, this is a shameful problem nationwide, but we would never do this in my school or district. Be careful; no one does this on purpose; that's why it's called unconscious bias.

At one such "never in my school" school, I led a discussion with the leadership team. First, I asked, "Do you ever have students who get sent to the office or suspended more often from math or English, but not other subjects?" As the team thought about some of the frequent offenders, an English teacher noted that one student, who never had a problem with her, was regularly sent out of math class. I pushed, "Do you think it's the subject or the teacher that's the variable?" Now everyone was looking at their hands, but not me. As the discussion continued, a few other teachers also noted that their students had challenges in math. After some simple data collection and analysis, they learned it wasn't the subject math, but the two math teachers that disproportionately sent students out of class.

In another instance at a large high school, three teachers accounted for 40 percent of suspensions. Just three teachers out of over a hundred fifty in the building. This isn't a problem with student behavior, but rather adult behavior, albeit unconscious and not ill intended. Next, the conversation with the "never at my school" leaders moved to racial disproportionality. Now, with relief, the school leaders shared that they had not been identified for disproportionate discipline by the state department of education.

They were surprised when I told them that this wasn't cause for celebration. Many states don't flag a school unless the disproportionality of suspensions is really high, say, three times the average. This means students of color could be 25 percent of the school, account for 74 percent of all suspensions, and still be under the threefold (3 x 25% = 75%) bar for official sanctions. This would be a school with serious issues, regardless of state accountability.

The first step in addressing unconscious bias is getting the data and owning them. Implementing safeguards as well as training are good next steps. A thoughtful codification of what constitutes disrespect or argumentative behavior helps create a common set of expectations. Perhaps the most stressful safeguard to implement is not allowing the handful of staff, if they exist, to continue to refer, detain, and suspend at rates three, ten, or even forty times their colleagues. This is not an easy conversation, but it's necessary.

Domain 4. Building trusting relationships between students and adults

Another key element of prevention-based SEB supports is building meaningful, trusting adult relationships with students. Students engage in their schoolwork more, behave better, seek and accept counseling support, and open up about their triggers when they believe at least one adult in the school cares about them as individuals and not just someone to educate, test, or punish.

> I've learned that people will forget what you said, people will forget what you did, but people will never forget how you made them feel.
>
> —CARL W. BUEHNER

Few educators feel this way about their students, but it's what the kids think that matters. Deterrence-based discipline, for example, is motivated by wanting to help, but it doesn't feel that way when you're on the receiving end of a detention or suspension. Even the three academic shifts outlined in the prior chapters are grounded in a desire to help kids be successful in life but can feel like a hyper-focus on test results, not the students themselves. Schools and districts can take proactive steps to ensure kids *do* know that the adults care for them as people as well as students.

Nearly all teachers I have met entered the field because they like and care about kids. So why is building relationships between staff and students such a front-burner issue in many schools today? There are a few reasons, but the two many districts need to address are the changing nature of students and the changing nature of the job.

The day when students were eager and ready to learn, were automatically engaged, and were respectful seems more like a Norman Rockwell painting than today's reality. Some veteran teachers long for the past, even if it wasn't fully true back in the day.

In many schools, current students differ from their teachers. The majority of students are black or brown, but the vast majority of teachers are not. Even in once overwhelmingly homogeneous schools, a third or more of students are often children of color.

As the kids have changed, so has the job. More public accountability for all kids to succeed, a heightened state focus on test scores, and larger classes due to smaller budgets puts a strain on teachers.

These changes create challenges on both sides of the relationship. A teacher can be overwhelmed in reaching out to a student who doesn't seem to care or who violently disrupted class yesterday. Kids who don't see teachers who look like themselves might not easily open up to them, and teachers without cultural literacy might not know how to reach out (or reach out appropriately). Finally, in a world that prizes a high level of academic skills, many teachers are focusing there first.

In this context, building trusting relationships is not simple, but is critical, academically and in preventing behavioral challenges. Districts can move forward in both structural and adaptive ways.

The structural or technical ways to facilitate the building of relationships are quicker but less impactful than the adaptive efforts. A structural solution is one that can be scheduled, staffed, mandated, or organized. It requires changes to the operations of the school, but not changes to the adults themselves. They can be a good place to start, but not a good place to end.

A simple start to the long-term process of seeing kids as individuals, not just students, is what I call the social data meeting. Many teachers have participated in data teams where they review student test results. Teachers know their students as learners, their strengths and academic gaps. The social data team meeting helps identify kids who have fallen through the cracks of caring adult relationships.

In large schools, especially high schools, sometimes staff don't know some students really well. If your first reaction is, "Not in my school; we know all our kids," then I encourage you to organize a social data meeting.

At a faculty or grade-level meeting, post a photo of each student (without their names) and list five questions before the images such as:

- What are their hobbies?
- What do they do after school or on weekends?
- What career interests do they have?
- What do their parent(s) do for work?
- Who are their closest friends?

Of course, each school should tweak the questions for relevance, but none should be related to the child's role as a student. Next, have teachers write answers on Post-it notes and place them under each photo next to the corresponding question. In about thirty minutes, you will see if any kids fall through the cracks when it comes to teachers knowing them as people. They are the ones for whom no one could answer some of the five questions.

> When asked to share their most positive learning experiences, a person would usually describe how certain key individuals touched his or her heart and mind. A teacher, coach, friend or family member's enthusiasm and passion for a subject left a strong impression. That same role model was trustworthy and believed in this person's strengths and capabilities even before they believed in them.[7]
>
> —JIM DILLON, AN EDUCATOR FOR OVER FORTY YEARS

Another structural change that helps build relationships is to encourage hallway small talk between teachers and all students by mandating that teachers hang out in the hallways during passing time. Students are very aware of what happens between class. Teachers who stay in their rooms or monitor the halls only to enforce deterrence discipline send the wrong message. Sure, teachers are busy, using the few minutes to plan for the next class, but their absence can unintentionally reinforce students' perception that no one cares. Conversely, asking about the game last night or their weekend is a powerful reminder that someone does care.

Small chats with kids can have a big impact. I remember a science teacher from middle school who routinely asked about my weekend. It was a lonely, sad time of my life as my mother wrestled, ultimately unsuccessfully, with cancer. Looking back, I don't know if this was spontaneous, generous outreach or a team meeting had highlighted my duress and assigned Mr. Weber to seek me out, but I do know that I remember these short conversations forty-five years later.

Selectively utilizing quick check-ins or checkouts for kids who doubt anybody cares, especially those who may have fallen through the cracks or are having a rough time, can help. A quick, planned, and structured chat at the start and end of the day goes a long way.

For thousands of years, relationships have been built over a meal. Once a week, a teacher could have lunch with a few students. Any topic of conservation except for grades, homework, and assignments is a good one. Students' choice of a teacher can supercharge this effort.

A lot of middle and high school principals frequently tell me that they have this covered, that every student in their school has an adult who cares about them, because every student has an advisory period each week. Unfortunately, this takes structural solutions too far. Simply putting twenty-five kids in a room with a teacher with the goal of forging a relationship isn't a guarantee that it will. Too often, kids are paired with teachers with whom they either share a problematic history or don't have much in common. Asking students who they want as an adviser can help, and sharing a teacher's background, hobbies, and interests before the selection can help kids make more informed choices.

Conceptually, many school leaders embrace more choice for kids, but fear upsetting the adults. One principal explained, "If we let kids pick their adviser, no one would ever pick Mr. Smith or Mrs. Jones. We can't have that." If that's true, then the students who are assigned to advisory period with these unpopular teachers are unlikely to suddenly feel that there is an adult who cares about them as a person.

The Des Moines public schools put high school students in the driver's seat to help build relationships and feel connected to school. They created a forum for students to give feedback to teachers on how to make classroom lessons more engaging and culturally relevant. Kids are the experts on what interests and is meaningful to them.

A 2017 Gallop education poll of students in grades five to twelve found only 47 percent of students were engaged in their school and learning. A disheartening 24 percent were actively disengaged. Building trusting relationships creates engagement and fertile soil for the three academic shifts to take root.[8]

FIRST, KNOW THYSELF. Socrates, Plato, and many others wrote that in order to connect with and understand others, first we must first know ourselves. Today's adaptive efforts to build trusting relationships with students, especially students from differing racial or social economic backgrounds, are guided by this sage advice.

A simple first step in this direction is to encourage teachers to think back to why they became teachers—to remember the teacher who took an interest in them or who found and developed a passion of theirs. In the hustle and bustle of being a teacher, among high-stakes accountability and the multitude of central office mandates, it's easy to lose sight of why folks became teachers in the first place. This reflection helps reorient the building of connections with kids from a structural solution to an urge to build a relationship.

Not everything we need to know about ourselves is as uplifting as recollections of high ideals from the past, however. Recognizing cultural illiteracy, privilege, and unconscious bias is also part of knowing thyself. And this is not fun or easy. Actually, it's nerve-wracking for many, but central to building relationships with kids, especially kids of color.

As a white man with much privilege, I'm not the best suited to address this challenge in many schools but avoiding the topic isn't part of the answer either. As schools and districts seek partners to help them build bridges, deepen understandings, and form close connections with students who aren't just like them, I can share a few lessons learned from others who have forded these rough waters.

Data help. Your own data help more. No amount of data helps enough. Many discussions about unconscious bias, for example, begin by sharing data. Facts and figures about access to AP and honors or discipline typically reveal racial bias. If the data are national, many people think "true, but not true here." If the data are districtwide, they think, "Sadly true, but not in my school." Collecting, analyzing, and sharing data that are directly connected to the staff is best. That said, although data might make one aware of a problem, they are seldom enough to change behavior.

A groundbreaking Boston Consulting Group study on private company efforts to tackle these issues can help guide schools as well. Two of the most important takeaways are that white men and woman can't lead the effort, and those who need to grow and change can't be shamed into improving. Both of these realities complicate the situation. In many districts, senior leaders are white; their support is critical, but their own biases and cultural illiteracies make them poorly suited for designing or screening effective programs.

Additionally, adaptive change has to be welcomed, not forced. Sometimes, efforts to help build awareness and skills in staff feel like a heavy dose of blame or accusation. Regardless of whether some shaming is deserved, the research indicates that shaming leads folks to shut down, get defensive, and not change.[9]

Domain 3. Mental health counseling, substance abuse support, and social work services

Not all kids come to school ready to learn. Key to helping these students is to provide substantive, high-quality mental health and substance abuse counseling. For some students, problematic behavior is rooted in anxiety, life stresses, substance issues, and such.

In many industrialized countries, state or municipal agencies provide free, high-quality mental health services to students (and others), but they frequently do not do so in the United States. As student mental health needs have grown, schools have responded the best they can. Districts hire a few social workers, another counselor, and maybe add a school psychologist. If they are cutting the budget due to limited revenue increases and rising health-care and pension costs, then even these modest steps are unaffordable. In some situations, many of these counselors and therapists are paid with special education funds and can't serve students without an IEP, despite the fact that over 50 percent of kids with mental health needs don't have an IEP. In order to help kids succeed in life, schools must address their mental health counseling needs with as much gusto and priority as their academic needs. Nearly, every parent, teacher, administrator, and school board member understands that kids need mental health counseling, but few know how to fund it. This challenge is addressed in the next chapter.

Domain 2. Social emotional competencies such as grit, empathy, and cooperation

All students, especially students who struggle, benefit from developing a wide range of SEL competencies. Skills and attributes such as grit, empathy, and cooperation will serve students well in the workplace, can minimize problematic behavior, and supercharge the academic best practices described in prior chapters.

Many wise folks have already weighed in on how best to teach and ingrain SEL competencies, including the Collaborative for Academic, Social, and Emotional Learning (CASEL) and the Aspen Institute. Their approach strongly embraces a focus on prevention.

The only addition to this great body of work is the caution to not confuse this domain with the other five domains. Each is important, but none are interchangeable. One school full of unhappy teachers makes the point. After much SEL PD, and a new lesson plan that infused cooperative learning, dealing with ambiguity, and empathy, the teachers were disappointed in the effort because it didn't reduce severe disruptive behaviors in their classrooms. They had mistakenly (or optimistically) assumed it would. Like all the domains, none is a cure-all.

Domain 1. Universal behavioral expectations and classroom routines

In my travels across the country, it seems to me that as a country, we are doing reasonably well in setting clear expectations and other tier-one universal norms, especially in elementary schools. I see documents, posters, PD, schoolwide assemblies, and the like. My spot quizzes with students in the hallway also suggest that most kids know what's expected and what behavior is in bounds and what is not.

New teachers welcome this clarity and direction. Despite decades of research and tears, new teachers receive little training in classroom management, a struggle that overwhelms many staff at the start of their careers. It often, sadly, leads to the premature end of their careers as well.

While middle schools and high schools are even more likely to have detailed written expectations for conduct, they are also less likely to have consistent, universal norms across the school because individual secondary classroom teachers have such great liberty to establish the rules of engagement. Drinking water in Mr. Fluentes's class is okay, but not in Ms. Green's. Eating a snack is cool with Ms. Ocassa, but Mr. O'Malley treats it as a criminal offense. Phones to take pictures of home assignments are required in one room and a cause for confiscation in the next.

In order to prevent kids from crossing the line, they need to know where the line is drawn. Some students (the "good ones") learn how to navigate teachers' different expectations, while others struggle to keep all the differing and conflicting rules straight. These kids aren't bad, but they are bad at steering a path through the maze of expectations.

STRUCTURE THE UNSTRUCTURED TIMES AS WELL. In many schools, PBIS, tier-one, or whole-school efforts work to make classrooms safe, supportive and welcoming spaces. Unfortunately, many of the most stressful moments happen or tensions begin to boil *outside* the classroom. Unstructured time on the bus, waiting for school to start, passing in the hallways, and during lunch or recess can be the source of much problematic behavior or anxiety.

On my visits, I've found it easy to identify which ones have focused on turning unstructured time into safe, calm spaces and which ones haven't yet. In some schools, teachers are in every doorway between periods to limit pushing, shoving, and bullying. You'll also hear teachers casually interacting with students, asking, "How was the game last night?" or "How was your weekend?" These simple interactions can help prevent bullying by reminding the would-be offender that someone really does care about them. In other schools, the hallways are chaotic, mean-spirited, and stressful, both psychologically as well as physically. Some schools have shortened passing time to just a minute or two or even instituted silent passing—no talking allowed.

A few readers may be thinking, "Kids can't get from one class to another in just two minutes, and it seems way too controlling to require silence in the hallways." Some schools have created clusters or houses so that most kids' classrooms are near one another; they reassigned teachers' rooms for the purpose of shortening passing time. And before you dismiss silent passing as cruel and unusual punishment, ask the kids being bullied or teased what they think is more desirable.

Less controversial is adding structure to recess. This includes having PE or classroom teachers organize games, having paraprofessionals closely monitor for shoving and teasing, mandating all-inclusive games, and creating safe spaces for kids to talk with caring adult supervisors nearby. Lunch with assigned seats, shortened to the time kids actually take to eat (a surprisingly short time), and allowing immediate access to supervised recess, all reduce the *Lord of the Flies* atmosphere that pervades some cafeterias every day.

Students can help themselves and each other during these times as well by making it easy to report problems or ask for help. Anonymous texting that bullying is going on adds strength to the "see something, say something" positive peer pressure posters omnipresent in many schools.

A BIG LIFT BUT WORTH THE EFFORT

Taken together, the six domains of SEB supports can help kids become better students and better people. They can help address social ills from outside the school walls and under the schoolhouse roof. They can ebb the flow of teacher burnout and, most importantly, help kids enjoy and flourish every day at school.

Most readers already know that few trends in K–12 have caught on so quickly and been adopted as widely. That said, teachers are telling anyone who will listen that something more is needed. Chapter 6 will show the way to better implementing these good ideas, especially in times of tight resources. Read on.

Improving Social, Emotional, and Behavioral Implementation

Getting Good at Doing Good

THE ADAGE "Doing the right thing the wrong way doesn't help kids" could be applied to any aspect of K–12, but this caution requires extra attention when it comes to the shift toward prevention and implementation of the six domains of SEB. Two factors contribute to the uber importance of effective implementation of SEB supports. The first is because this is relatively new territory for most schools, and the second is because implementation of prevention efforts often gets less attention than other, more academic-focused efforts.

Most schools have been refining their approach to teaching reading, math, writing, and so on for decades. The craft of teaching has been studied, discussed, refined, and aided by instructional coaches as well. The shift to prevention doesn't have as long a track record. Thus, many schools are still new at figuring out how best to deliver SEB services. School-based SEB is an emerging field, likely to be implemented less than perfectly at first.

In my travels, I've seen SEB and prevention efforts measured and managed with *less* rigor than academic program rollouts, despite the greater need to learn, experiment, and refine. The most telling proof point of this is that a disconnect can be gleaned from even a short conversation with nearly any classroom teacher.

When I speak with central office leaders and principals, they often proudly share the thoughtful efforts they have implemented that shift the focus to prevention, including adding behavior specialists, teaching social emotional skills, and fostering student-teacher relationships. They beam proudly as they detail research-based, thoughtful plans. Their joy stands in stark contrast with the near universal clamor from frontline teachers asking for more staff, more programs, more strategies—in short, more help.

My experience is that while the central office–developed plans have been solid, the implementation hasn't been, leaving teachers wanting more. In many situations, improving implementation of current efforts is a better next step than starting something new or simply hoping that throwing more staff at the problem might solve it.

BEING SOFT?

Before districts can effectively shift to a focus on prevention, they have to be ready for the new approach. One of the most common reasons such efforts fail is because too many teachers and principals worry that the shift to prevention is being soft and will likely lead to an even worse situation. They fear that it gives a free pass to kids who don't obey the rules and perhaps coddles kids who deserve a harsh reaction.

If you or your staff are feeling this way, then you're not ready to implement a prevention-based approach. This is most obvious related to domain six, managing severe behaviors. Note to district leaders: don't force this best practice–based approach to SEB on schools that aren't ready to embrace it. It doesn't end well. Before schools and districts are ready to embrace prevention, including deterrence for many and building coping and avoidance skills to prevent triggers for some, staff need to wrestle with three philosophical questions:

- Can students control their behavior?
- Can adults help students control their behavior?
- Is it fair that some students are treated differently than others?

Only when a majority of staff sincerely believe:

- Yes, most students can control their behavior, but some cannot.
- It's hard, but yes, as teachers, we can help nearly all students learn to control their problematic behavior when guided by a behavior specialist. We realize that we may be unintentionally triggering much of our students' most problematic behavior as well, even though this was never our intention.
- Yes, we should provide the supports each student needs; that's fair. Just as academic supports differ by student need, so should behavior supports and discipline actions. Equity doesn't mean equality; it means helping based on individual student needs.

Teachers find the second question emotionally hard, but with the help of a skilled behaviorist, they accept it quickly. However, the third question, about fairness, seems to rile a lot of people.

In one school, a student I'll call Darnell, had very problematic behavior but was on a good path forward. Through the help of a talented behaviorist, they identified his triggers, developed coping mechanisms, and prevented outbursts, thanks also to much effort by the classroom teacher. Things weren't perfect, but daily problems were reduced to weekly events. One component of the mitigation plan was that, when Darnell felt an outburst coming, he would stand up, immediately leave the room, walk two laps around the corridor, breathing slowly along the way, and then return and sit down. During one such self-directed prevention walk, he was approached by the assistant principal (AP).

AP: Darnell, where is your hall pass?

DARNELL: I don't need one. I'm coping right grow. It's part of my plan.

AP: Where is your hall pass? (*a bit louder*)

DARNELL: I don't need one! (*louder*)

AP: Everyone needs a hall pass. We can't allow students to wander the halls whenever they want. That's not fair. We explained the rules at the start of year assembly. Don't you remember?

DARNELL: I'M NOT LYING! I DON'T NEED A PASS AND YOU ARE STUPID! (*very loud*)

AP: Darnell, that's unacceptable language. Come to my office with me. (*sternly*)

DARNELL: No, I HAVE to go to class! (*very agitated*)

Yes, he did push the assistant principal and did get suspended for three days. But, no, Darnell would not be deterred from future similar interactions by the suspension. He behaved as best he knew how.

A shift to prevention, especially for students with the most severe behavioral challenges, requires a belief that some kids lack certain skills and, as such, they need carefully crafted accommodations to the discipline code.

To be clear, student and teacher safety are paramount and should never be sacrificed in any behavior plan. Nor does a focus on prevention require or even suggest a prohibition on suspensions or expulsions. Sometimes, districts go too far in trying to embrace prevention by virtually prohibiting or greatly restricting suspension or expulsion.

Like almost everything in life, finding the right balance is the key. Safety is paramount, and deterrence is still appropriate for many students. Perhaps the most worrisome side effect of moving too fast toward reducing suspensions and expulsions is that it backfires, and good efforts are stopped dead in their tracks. This can happen when the pendulum swings too far, as K–12 schools are fond of doing. One district, which oversuspended and expelled students of color, took thoughtful steps to address this shortcoming but went too far. It quickly returned to the classroom students who had hurt teachers or posed serious threats to school safety . Teachers and their association swarmed the school board, the press, and faculty meetings. In relatively short order, the superintendent was gone, and with her, the efforts to right a wrong.

Perhaps even more worrisome is that the perception of safety matters as much as actual safety. One district made great strides in reducing suspensions and expulsions, and at the same time, the number of unsafe or problematic behavior events also dropped. This should have been a success story, but it wasn't. The district hadn't had key conversations with staff and hadn't wrestled with the hard issues. While the schools did actually become safer, the perception was different. Confirmation bias, the tendency to see what we expect to see, led many teachers to believe that life at work had become more dangerous. They lobbied hard and successfully to go back to the old ways. While students and climate suffered, the teachers felt much safer.

THREE LESSONS FROM THE FIELD

So what does improving implementation of SEB look like exactly? The following are some important lessons I've learned from the more successful districts across the country:

1. *Focus; don't do too much at once.* There is so much to do to meet all the needs of today's students. All six domains are worthwhile and desperately needed. That said, no district has the bandwidth to tackle all six at once and implement them well.
2. *Don't overload the staff.* Student needs are significant, and staffing levels never seem to be enough. Stretching current staff thin to meet the ever-expanding needs leads to stress, burnout, and fewer services, not more. Thoughtful strategies for helping teachers better handle the workload and expanding their ranks through community partnerships will help kids and teachers alike.
3. *Don't assume success; measure and adjust.* Good ideas backed by good plans should be effective. Unfortunately, they aren't always home runs. Only by measuring actual impact and adjusting accordingly can SEB plans fulfill their potential.

1. Focus on just a few things

Managing behaviors, preventing outbursts, building relationships, supporting outside partners, and instilling grit and empathy are all complicated efforts. None are simple to implement. To complicate matters further, some efforts have three tiers, which each brings its own set of complications. Lastly, each level (elementary, middle, and high school) requires nuanced differences in implementation.

Many schools conduct a *needs* assessment to guide their SEB work. This seems like a good practice, but a *prioritization* assessment can lead to better implementation. What's the difference between needs and prioritization assessments? The first answers the question, "What is worth doing?" and the second answers, "What should we do first?"

Let's run some numbers to highlight the differences. What might be worth implementing? A needs assessment might yield six areas requiring attention. That's a lot, but not unrealistic given the changing profile of today's students. Maybe a district can tackle all or most of these. Maybe it focuses on only the first four.

A closer look, however, reveals that implementing any of these requires a different plan at the elementary, middle, and high school levels. So, there are not six things to implement but eighteen. But look more closely. Behavior management isn't one effort but one for each of the three tiers. The list of six grows to thirty-nine. No district can implement thirty-nine hard, paradigm-shifting efforts at once, but far too many try. Worse yet, they don't create separate plans for each level and tier, because they don't have the bandwidth. (See table 6.1.)

While everything on this list is worthwhile, thirty-nine efforts are too many to effectively implement all at once. Prioritization forces you to select just two or three efforts, such as tier-two behavior management at the high school level or tier-three mental health supports at the elementary level. It's hard to say no (for now) to so many other worthwhile efforts, but teachers and kids all need these efforts to be well implemented.

DISTRICTWIDE EFFORTS HELP CREATE FOCUS. One way to increase focus and improve implementation is to tackle SEB challenges as a district, not

TABLE 6.1

Example of needs assessment

Needs	School levels	RELEVANT TIERS			Total tiers	Discrete efforts
		Tier 1	Tier 2	Tier 3		
Behavior management	3	X	X	X	3	9
School norms	3	X	X		2	6
Empathy	3	X	X		2	6
Collaboration	3	X			1	3
Cultural understanding	3	X	X		2	6
Mental health services	3	X	X	X	3	9
Total efforts requiring planning and implementation						39

school by school. In many districts, each school develops its own approach and priorities for managing behavior and instilling SEL skills. This makes sense because the schools are quick to identify the need, and needs can vary from school to school within a district. While logical, it's also often less effective, not because central offices are more capable of implementing SEB plans well, but because schools typically lack the span of control and authority needed to effectively implement them.

Whether it's changing discipline policies, altering hiring practices, realigning resources, or reducing some existing content to make way for SEL direct instruction, schools often can't implement the necessary changes without permission at the district level. District leaders have the clout and authority, but are reluctant to make exceptions for one school, but not another. A districtwide approach bridges this gap.

Focus helps beyond just limiting the stress on bandwidth for change. It also forces planners to target specific tiers and create plans in a more nuanced way for each tier. Thanks to widespread adoption of RTI/MTSS, we all know about the tiers. Tier one is universal (for everyone), tier two is for the 10 to 15 percent of kids with greater needs, and tier three is for the 3 to 5 percent of students with the greatest challenges. Managing behaviors, instilling SEL competencies, or building relationships also follows the tiers. This, too, is widely understood, but too often in practice, the tiers get blurred during implementation. Tier-one strategies are used for tier-three challenges, or tier-three supports are applied to tier-two needs, for example. This often occurs because the district doesn't build out three distinct efforts, one for each tier. It's a case of "if all you have is a hammer, everything starts to look like a nail."

I have seen a perfectly good tier-two intervention, such as restorative justice circles—a student telling a friend how it feels to be teased—applied to an extreme case of a student throwing scissors at a teacher. A good strategy, misapplied. After being grazed by a sharp projectile, teachers expect more than a calm conversation about feelings with a student. Some districts I visit utilize very time-consuming tier-three trigger explorations with every tier-two incident, quickly overwhelming the behavior support staff.

Doing a few things well is a whole lot better than doing many things not so well. The heart may say do it all, but that's not the kindest path forward.

2. Don't overload the staff

School and district leaders seem stuck with a Sophie's choice. Keep the workload of SEB staff reasonable, but let some students go underserved, or prioritize meeting the ever-expanding needs of kids and hope that school psychologists, counselors, behaviorists, and social workers go the extra mile or two.

You may be saying to yourself, "Nice idea to not overload the staff, but with our budget, it's not practical to add sufficient mental health and behavior specialists to meet all the needs." Here are some ideas for getting first-class support on a limited budget and not burning out great folks in the process.

MAXIMIZE THE IMPACT OF CURRENT STAFF BY STREAMLINING PROCESS AND PAPERWORK. Many school psychologists have the skill and training to provide counseling, but often there is little time in the day for counseling after all the evaluations, testing, and report writing. Because IEP evaluation work is mandated, counseling is relegated to the leftover time.

Wouldn't it be great if the paperwork and the IEP process could be streamlined to free up time for counseling? While nearly all school psychologists and their leaders believe they are efficient and take a typical amount of time for each task, the truth is startling. While every school in the United States has a relatively similar workflow—including referral → evaluation → report writing → IEP meeting → IEP finalized—the time and detailed tasks vary greatly from district to district and even from one staff member to another in the same district.

Nine districts, neighboring each other, asked my firm to determine how many hours of work it took to complete the IEP process from start to finish. They assumed the answers would be quite similar, but in fact, one district spent thirty-seven hours per evaluation, while another took just twelve, on average. There was no "normal," as the data in figure 6.1 show. The surprises didn't stop there. Within a single district, some folks were 50 percent quicker than others.

FIGURE 6.1

Time per initial or three-year evaluation

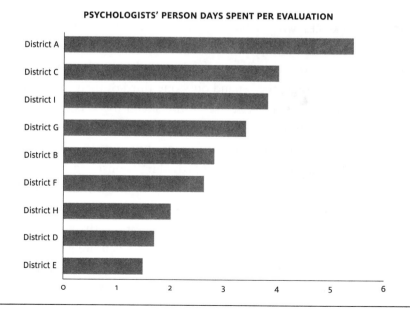

PSYCHOLOGISTS' PERSON DAYS SPENT PER EVALUATION

Each district's history, culture, preferences, interpretation of the law, and customs dictated how long it took to go through all the legally mandated steps of determining eligibility and creating the IEP. The power of school culture and district norms was so strong, that other studies indicated that if a school psychologist who went through the process quite quickly moved to a new district in the same state where the process was much slower, on average, the psychologist would soon take as long as the new district average. Seven years of doing it one way, a quick and compliant way, changed within a few months, now took more than three times longer. What was most shocking was that no one ever sat down with the new employee and explained the process. She just inferred the new approach and wanted to fit in.

Through the science of process mapping, some schools have reduced the time to do a thorough initial or three-year evaluation by 25 percent or even 60 percent. (See the sidebar "Process Mapping Streamlines Meetings and Paperwork.") Every minute saved is a minute of additional counseling. It's a lot easier to free up the time of existing staff than to find the funds for new school psychologists.

PRIORITIZE SERVICES WITH STUDENTS OVER MEETINGS. Meetings are important, but how many are too many? Social workers in many districts spend most of their day with other adults, rather than working with kids. On average, they spend only one-third of their day with students, based on time studies of over 1,400 social workers in more than 125 districts. In comparison, if these same talented folks worked for a local counseling agency or were in private practice, they would typically spend 85 percent of their time providing counseling.

Most school-based social workers want to work more with kids. Few counselors enter the field due to their love of meetings. Others in the school, however, often invite them to lots of meetings, and administrators often expect them to attend as well. It's definitely nice to have a social worker at IEP meetings, team meetings, RTI meetings, student support meetings, and the like. Each invitation eats up just thirty

PROCESS MAPPING STREAMLINES
MEETINGS AND PAPERWORK

Many special education staff and leaders wish they could streamline meetings and paperwork, but few believe they can. Process mapping is a structured way to stream-line. Five steps free up more time to work with students. This process is inclusive, conducted with staff, not to them.

1. Identify All the Steps, in Fine Detail

For each of the most common processes, such as creating a three-year initial IEP, list each step in fine detail. Every meeting needed, every call typically made (include the calls that aren't answered or returned), every assessment given, and so on. The more detail, the better. For example, don't list "give assessment" as a task, but rather dis-sect this one task into its parts, such as select the assessment, administer the assess-ment, score, and write summaries. You can't go into too much detail. Listing which modules of each assessment is used also sheds light on the process, revealing op-portunities in the subsequent steps. For each step, also list who is in the room when the task is being done.

2. Ask the Exclusion Questions

For each task, critically assess whether it and everyone involved with it is absolutely necessary.

- Can this step be eliminated completely?
- Can this step be eliminated in some instances? Perhaps for speech-only IEPs or for students with only academic needs or for students making solid progress.
- Can some participants skip the meeting?
- Can some participants leave the meeting early?
- In which situations could someone skip the meeting?

When answering the questions, the litmus test isn't whether it is valuable to do the task or attend the meeting but, rather, is it *more* valuable than working with students?

The process of answering these questions often benefits from having an out-side facilitator. Remember, every step is being done because someone in the past thought it was a good idea. The most common challenge to this step is that some in the room will believe the law requires a step (even though it doesn't), that leader-ship wants it (even though that leader might have left the district years ago), or it is really important sometimes (even though the question encourages doing it some-times rather than always).

(continues)

3. Individually Estimate Time Required for Each Task or Meeting

Some districts do detailed time studies for a few weeks; others simply ask each practitioner to estimate on their own.

4. Learn from the Quickest

Often there will be a few people in the room who can do a task (like giving eligibility assessments) much faster than others—not just 10 percent faster, but five times quicker. They have learned a software shortcut, skip steps in certain cases, or meet the requirements in a different way. Seldom do they do the same tasks quicker; they do them differently.

5. Investigate, Don't Dismiss, Options to Streamline

By the end of step four, it's common for many to feel that the shortcuts or changes surfaced are either illegal or that district leadership won't support them. Both concerns are often unwarranted, and senior leadership needs to clearly resolve these concerns and unambiguously give permission to make the changes. If any doubt remains that the changes will violate the law or expectations, they are unlikely to ever be implemented.

This approach to process mapping can often free up five to ten hours of additional time with students each week, improve staff morale, all while maintaining 100 percent compliance.

minutes or an hour, so it may not seem like much time. When twenty such invitations come each week, it is quite a lot.

Counseling happens in the leftover time between the meetings. One district where lots of meetings meant just 25 percent of the day went to counseling proactively prioritized therapy. It formally set the expectation that 75 percent of the day would go to direct service with students, and meetings had to fit in the balance. After only a few weeks, folks prioritized which meetings they attended and how long they stayed. Counseling services tripled without adding a single new person. The social workers' morale also increased because they became empowered to say, "Sorry, I'd love to attend the meeting, but that time is reserved for working with students."

LET THE MOST-SKILLED COUNSELORS COUNSEL. Most districts ask school psychologists, counselors, and others to do a zillion other things, such as assess students for eligibility, chair the IEP process, ensure timeline compliance, and so on. While these tasks can be streamlined, they won't ever go away completely. Rather than asking every school psychologist to do some counseling and lots of other tasks, kids and staff benefit when the most well-trained folks mostly do counseling, and other school psychologists with less training and interest in counseling handle the noncounseling activities. This increases the availability of high-quality counseling services while improving staff morale, as everyone is playing to their strengths and passions.

If you think putting all the paperwork on just a few folks is unfair, think again. In district after district, when such positions have been posted, more than enough current staff members apply with glee. Some people really like this work; others don't.

SEEK OUT BEHAVIOR SPECIALISTS WHO ARE TRULY SPECIALISTS. Managing problematic behavior is a science, one that some people train and study to master. Many schools are adding these highly desirable positions, but with mixed results. It turns out that sometimes the behavior specialists aren't expert in managing problematic behaviors with a focus on prevention. This mismatch of title and skill happens in a few ways. Sometimes the hiring committee assumes everyone with the title or certification of school psychologist or counselor is, in fact, an expert at managing behaviors. *Some* of these folks have extensive behavior management training, while others have different skills.

In one district, for example, every school was to be staffed with a behavior specialist as part of a major effort to help address tier-three behavior challenges. Kudos to the district for prioritizing the need and funding a significant expansion in staffing. Staff anger rather than appreciation followed. A principal sadly explained, "Our behavior specialist was nervous around kids, wasn't sure what to do, but really wanted to help. She asked me how best to handle students with severe behaviors, but I didn't know what to do, that . . . was her job." It turns out the district had simply reassigned a portion of its existing school psychologists as school-based behavior specialists. It had assumed all school psychologists were behavior experts.

Given the evolving role of social psychologists over the decades, it's easy to understand why simply having the title doesn't indicate whether they are actually trained and comfortable in helping to manage behavior, but oddly enough, even staff with the title and training of behavior specialist are not experts at preventing behavioral outbursts or identifying the associated triggers. Not all people called behavior specialists can help classroom teachers and kids better manage challenging behaviors.

A very unhappy principal brought this oddity to my attention. His school had hired a certified behavior specialist, yet the situation didn't improve; worse yet, classroom teachers seemed to be *more* stressed. This surprised me, so I spent some time with the newly hired behavior expert. She was smart, hardworking, well trained, but trained differently.

Behavior experts come in different flavors. To oversimplify (I'm describing extremes to make a point), some behaviorists focus on identifying triggers, mitigating them, and helping teachers and students avoid them. Others focus more on tracking data related to problematic behavior, noting trends, and creating incentives to encourage better behavior, and then track if the incentives are effective. Unfortunately, this approach often pushes data collection to the teacher (thus, greater stress) and focuses less on identifying triggers by understanding a student's inner monologue. This second flavor of behaviorist has its roots in specialized classrooms, often for students on the autism spectrum. While many effective behaviorists use a mix of these two approaches, strength in identifying triggers is key to focusing on prevention.

CONSIDER SMALL GROUPS. Another impactful way to extend the reach of talented mental health and counseling staff is to encourage small-group counseling when appropriate. There exists a disconnect between in-school and out-of-school mental health and substance abuse services. Based on our extensive review of the schedules of district-employed staff, the most mental health services are provided one on one—one staff member helping one student at a time. It's so widespread that few schools ever consider anything else. When they discuss the topic, more than a few fear that small-group counseling is unethical or illegal or violates privacy norms. That said, many non-school-based providers often combine some one-on-one sessions with group sessions. These practitioners reason that there is value in hearing from others, knowing your issues aren't unique, gaining support from peers or even positive per pressure for accountability. Small groups also leverage limited and talented staff.

A simple example makes the case. Assume one FTE counselor holds twenty-one-hour sessions a week. If all are one-one-one sessions, then the counselor provides twenty student hours of counseling. (A student hour is the number of hours students receive counseling, e.g., two students in a group for an hour is two student hours of counseling.) If the same FTE counselor scheduled half of the counseling one on one, and half were small groups of four, then the counselor would deliver fifty student hours of services. This small change, a commonplace practice outside schools, is the same as adding a 1.5 additional FTE to the current model. Few schools have the resources to increase counseling staffing by 150 percent, but most could increase student hours of counseling by this amount. Group services aren't right for every student or every need but are worth a serious review.

EXPAND COMMUNITY PARTNERSHIPS. School budgets will likely never support all the mental health and counseling needs of today's students, even if all the ideas previously shared for expanding the reach of existing staff are implemented well. Even if budgets grow, the typical school district culture and pay scale might never appeal to all the talented experts needed as well. But this is okay. Districts can access lots of outside, talented staff at little cost by expanding community-based partnerships.

Fortunately, many communities have nonprofit counseling centers, fee-for-service psychologists, independent practitioner social workers, and community-funded mental health clinics or hospitals that can help meet the need for highly skilled mental health services.

Third-party providers can be a great addition to supplement a district's own staff. They bring specialized expertise, have the ability to work with families as well as students, are connected to other non-school services, and can be free or low-cost because someone else pays. Sometimes, as in the case of nonprofit counseling agencies, their own budgets fund the work. In the case of university training programs, student tuition foots the bill, and for many fee-for-service providers or local clinics, student insurance covers the cost.

If you are thinking, "We do this already," don't skip ahead until you take the following simple test. Many districts do this, but far fewer do it at scale or at little or no cost.

QUIZ

Have you maximized third-party mental health services? You will need to gather three bits of data:

A. Total student enrollment in the district.
B. An approximation of the value of services from third parties like community-based counselors, nonprofit clinics, or fee-for-service providers. It's the sum of what they would charge typical clients. A quick alternative way to calculate the value of services received is to multiply the FTE of staff time provided times the average salary with benefits of a teacher in the district. If you're not sure of this figure, just use $75,000 as a rough national average.
C. The cost the district actually pays for these services. It's zero if they are provided for free. If they are billed to the district, it's the sum of annual invoices.

Now let's calculate the amount of free mental health services received per 1,000 students:

$$\text{Free services per 1,000 students} = \frac{(B - C) * (1{,}000)}{A}$$

For example:

A = 5,000 students
B = 20 FTE of third-party providers, thus 20 x $75,000 = $1,500,000
C = Cost to district = $50,000 a year

$$\textbf{Free services per 1,000 students} = \frac{(\$1{,}500{,}000 - \$50{,}000)\,(1{,}000)}{5{,}000}$$
$$= \$290{,}000$$

Now let's see how well your district is maximizing the potential of high-quality, paid-by-others mental health services.

Free services per 1,000 students	Rating
Less than $10,000	Time to get started
$10,000—$100,000	Good start, now build on it
$100,000—$250,000	Well done, but what's next?
More than $250,000	You're ready to show others how

A close look at districts that receive a lot of free or low-cost, highly skilled mental health services reveals a few common themes to their success. Collectively, these themes sum up to "Make your schools a great place for community-based partners to work!"

Based on focus groups with these desperately needed, great-to-have providers, I've found that often the opposite is true. Whether it's small things like no place to put a coat and purse, indignities like student schedules being changed without notification, or economic disincentives like dead time between appointments or sloppy paperwork impacting insurance reimbursement, some schools just aren't making it fun or easy for outsiders to fit in. The most successful districts have all of the following:

- *Dedicated leadership.* Someone with authority and time identifies, courts, supports, and manages outside partners. This differs greatly from tasking already overloaded principals or heads of guidance or special education with the responsibility. For a district of five thousand students, for example, fifteen to twenty hours per week of a leader's time is a reasonable investment and can be expected to yield $1 million of services.
- *A school schedule aligned to the outside world.* All nonschool organizations work a Monday to Friday schedule. Standing meetings happen at the same time each week, say, Monday at 9:00 a.m. Some schools have similar structures, but not all. Rotating schedules, drop periods (each day has just six of seven periods), A/B (every other day's schedule is different) schedules,

and schedules that change due to snow days or other events make it very hard for third-party practitioners to integrate school-based work and their other responsibilities.

- *High-quality space.* Counseling sessions are held in clean, appropriately sized rooms with privacy. Counselors also have a place to hang their coats and secure their valuables. Nothing says, "We don't really value you" more than giving third-party providers the worst space in the school. If good space isn't available, high-quality portable space, renting for about $30,000 a year, can house $250,000 of otherwise free services at a high school, for example.

- *Real-time problem solving.* Every session is precious, and when problems or conflicts occur, solutions are needed in minutes, not weeks. If a therapy room is already occupied, a substitute teacher says a student must stay for a quiz, or a multitude of other things goes wrong, they are addressed quickly. Too often, the third-party practitioner walks to the principal's office, the secretary can't solve the issue, and the principal is tied up. The session will end before the glitch is resolved, and frustration grows. More successful efforts have instant resolution by providing text access to a leader who has the clout to resolve the issue immediately.

- *Close integration with school and district staff.* Third-party providers want to feel part of the school and district. They need to be as well in order to maximize their effectiveness. They should be invited to join facility meetings and regularly scheduled for at-risk student meetings.

- *An investment mentality.* Perhaps the biggest difference between districts with some community-based partnership services and many services is an investment mind-set. They believe that expending time, money, and political capital to do the above-mentioned best practices will pay off for kids and the budget.

Too often I hear pushback like, "We could never pay an administrator to oversee nondistrict staff," or "The teachers would be angry if we got rid of the rotating schedule," or "We have to give our best space to our people." Strangely, these same districts find the money for out-of-district placements or a single new staff member, or change the schedule when a new principal is hired. None of these best practices is easy or pain free, but they are worth the cost.

3. Don't assume success; measure and adjust

The most effective SEB implementers rigorously measure the impact of their efforts. Many people may be surprised by this, since behavior, SEL competencies, and trusting relationships aren't well suited for standardized tests. Moreover, many of the strongest proponents of SEB efforts are, at times, jaded by federal and state testing regimens. Anything worth doing, however, is worth measuring, and doing anything well usually requires good measures.

Okay, but how do you measure the impact of an antibullying tier-one effort or a tier-two undertaking to build relationships with students? I'm asked these questions a lot, because unlike many other data points, schools and districts don't have this data at their fingertips. Districts collect the data that the state, the federal government, or the board mandates.

This means districts must proactively collect baseline data and then track progress with district-developed tools. Usually these involve carefully crafting student surveys and other student feedback mechanisms. For example, want to know if the tier-one antibullying program is working? Ask all students, through an anonymous survey, "Have you been teased, harassed, or bullied in the last month?" Ask every four months and see if the numbers decrease. Want to know if an advisory period is helping kids feel connected to school? Take the list of students who fell through the cracks from the exercise in the previous chapter and text them a single question every few months, such as, "Is there an adult who cares about you in the school?" or "Does any teacher know your interests outside of school?" Unfortunately, many schools are disappointed with the data, but they will know it's time to improve the implementation.

Once the data come back, celebrate success and take action to refine as needed. If the data are disappointing, it's critical to check if the effort was well implemented, with fidelity, before abandoning the effort and trying something else. The most common reason thoughtful SEB plans don't deliver the desired results is inadequate implementation, not ill-conceived planning. Figure 6.2 outlines the implementation prerequisites that need to be in place before positive impact can be expected.

Another very common area of adjustment is whatever is adjacent to the SEB effort itself. SEB efforts don't exist in a vacuum. In fact, they interact with myriad aspects of a school and district. Does the

FIGURE 6.2
SEB implementation prerequisites

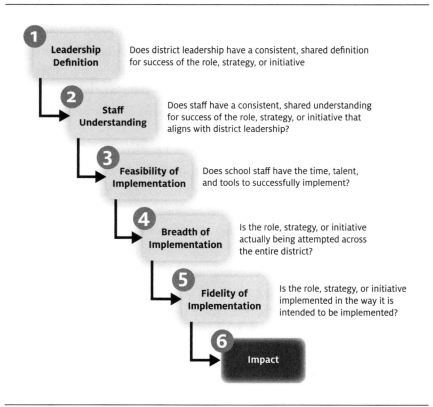

FIGURE 6.3

Misalignment of SEB strategy and existing systems and policies

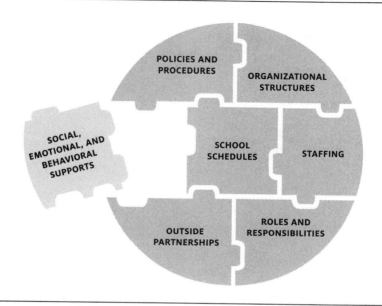

discipline policy support tier-three behavior trigger prevention? Does the budget support a part-time director of external partnerships? Does the elementary master schedule make time for whole-class tier-one direct instruction in school norms? And so much more.

Effective implementation requires identifying all the interconnections between the prioritized efforts and other policies and practices. It ends with thoughtful redesign of the ecosystem to support the efforts. (See figure 6.3.)

• • • • • • • • • • • • • • • • •

Kids and teachers desperately need more and better SEB supports and services. The hardest part of meeting these needs will be to balance the desire to achieve that with the reality that few schools and districts have the capacity to address every need at once. And while staff want to give it their all, if leaders ask for too much, they risk losing the very folks they need so greatly.

Harder yet is that only a clear-eyed, objective measure of success will guide the refinement of each effort. Much of SEB services pull at our hearts, but cold, methodical, thoughtful implementation is the kindest gift we can give to students.

CHAPTER 7

Shift #5: From One Good Schedule to Many Great Schedules

Don't skip this chapter! If you're thinking that I'm interested in raising achievement for kids who struggle, that I'm motivated by meeting the social, emotional, and behavioral needs of kids, and that I want to update special education for a new era, and I don't really care to learn much about scheduling, I don't blame you. I came to appreciate the importance of scheduling in a very roundabout way. For the longest time, I didn't care at all about scheduling. It seemed tactical, tedious, and not very important. I was very wrong.

Effectively implementing any of the other desired shifts in practice without treating scheduling as strategically important is nearly impossible. It is a critical tool for better serving kids who struggle, both with and without special needs. One of the most common reasons districts don't implement the four shifts I've shared so far is because they try to shoehorn the new approaches and strategies into the old schedule.

The links between scheduling and improved academic achievement and better SEB supports are vast. I hope they are evident after you've read the prior chapters, but let's recap the interconnections:

- Never pull students from core ELA and math instruction to get supplemental services. Based on my firm's studies, over 50 percent of students are pulled from core reading for extra help. This, of course, isn't extra; it's just instead of. Students are also commonly pulled from math or reading to get speech and language or occupational therapy services.

- Group students who receive extra help or related services based on similar areas of need. Most often they are grouped based having the same homeroom teacher.
- Provide intervention every day, not just on the days that it can be scheduled.
- Provide double time in math, ELA, or reading for struggling students.
- Provide intervention to 100 percent of students who qualify, not just those who can be fit into the relevant teacher's schedule.
- Maximize special educators' time with students to the extent practical.
- Maximize time committed to counseling for SEB staff like social workers, counselors, and school psychologists.
- Provide time for teacher collaboration.
- Ensure that instructional coaches are supporting teachers most of the day and can join many common planning sessions each week.
- Include time in the day for direct instruction in social and emotional learning.
- Include time in the week for building trusting relationships.

Two things to note when reviewing this list. It is a long list and it contains many different types of schedules to manage. To effectively and cost effectively implement the best practices for serving struggling students, a whole lot of schedules need to support these shifts in practice. At the elementary level, this includes master building schedules and the schedules of every reading teacher, special educator, related service provider, interventionists, paraprofessionals, instructional coaches, school psychologists, social workers, and counselors. At the secondary level, double time with content-strong teachers requires new schedules for both teachers and students.

THE EVOLUTION OF SCHEDULING

Schedules are important because they guide how a very precious resource, time, is used. Most school systems have already started to treat scheduling as more important than in the past. Gone are the days when an elementary master schedule only listed when art, lunch, and recess took place. The rest was left up to each teacher to decide on their own.

One study I conducted more than a decade ago indicates what was typical of scheduling for the era. One-third of elementary teachers across the district dedicated thirty minutes a day to math, one-third devoted forty-five minutes each day, and only one-third committed a full hour to math. The program, unambiguously, required sixty minutes a day simply to cover all the chapters in the math textbook. Today's elementary schedules address this head-on. The most common elementary schedules across the country spell out specific time commitments for reading, math, science, social studies, and, of course, lunch, recess, and specials.

While a step in the right direction, these schedules do not scream that reading is the foundation to all other learning and that all struggling students must read at grade level or their lives will be irreparably harmed. What's missing? The details of how reading will be taught and when extra time to learn will be provided. Based on hundreds of interviews and reviews of thousands of schedules, I have found that a lot is still left up to classroom teachers to figure out:

- Is writing part of the ninety-minute reading block or in addition to? In some schools, no one seemed sure, and each teacher made his or her own best guess.
- How much time should be devoted to phonics each day? Within the same school, it can range from a few minutes to half an hour each day.
- In what grades will phonics be taught to all students? Some second-grade teachers don't think it's age appropriate, while others do.

- How much time will be devoted to small-group instruction?
- When will intervention happen?

Great schedules clearly spell out answers to all these questions. This shouldn't be a top-down directive, but rather developed in partnership with teachers; it should be consistent and support the best practices. Overwhelming evidence has emerged that few schools fully implement the What Works Clearinghouse and National Reading Panel best practices.[1] Better, more detailed schedules can help rectify this shortcoming. (See figure 7.1.)

Crafting the best allocation of time during the day isn't easy. Those in the central office, directors of teaching and learning, or folks with similar titles often take up the challenge, but sometimes fail to address head-on the stark reality that they need to make unpopular decisions and tough trade-offs.

FIGURE 7.1
The evolution of elementary scheduling

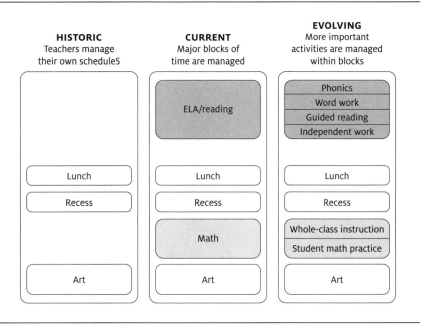

Please, don't schedule more than what can fit in the day. About half the lists of recommended instructional minutes I have reviewed actually add up to more minutes than the school day. A simple tally shows 480 minutes of requirements in a 450-minute day, for example. Unwilling or unable to decide what to trim to add intervention, dedicated writing, or SEL instruction, some have simply added without subtracting. Obviously, this is discouraging to teachers; they revert back to doing what they think is best.

THE RIGHT ANSWER TO THE WRONG QUESTION

There is one tough question that leaders can dodge. The most common question I'm asked about scheduling is which type of secondary schedule is best? Is a block schedule better? Do seven periods or eight raise achievement? Do rotating schedules help struggling students? Research says these aren't the important questions.[2] A hundred percent of core instruction, plus extra time with a content-strong teacher, helps most and can fit into nearly any form of schedule.

Great schedules start with clear non-negotiables

"I love my schedule!" Actually, I have never heard anyone proclaim this level of affection for a schedule. Typically, a schedule is an uncomfortable compromise between less than perfect trade-offs. The inherent complexity of building schedules always leads to some disappointment.

As master schedulers are quick to say, "You can schedule anything, just not everything." The first step in building great schedules is to state up front what would make a schedule great. This might seem a simplistic idea, but it's revolutionary. This lets you know when it's okay to finalize the schedule. (See the sidebar "What Makes a Great Elementary School Schedule?" for some thoughts on best practice aligned non-negotiables.) It turns scheduling into a criterion-based exercise that doesn't end until all the student-centered, best-practice-based non-negotiables are met, rather than simply being the best schedule that seemed possible, warts and all. It transforms scheduling from

WHAT MAKES A GREAT ELEMENTARY SCHOOL SCHEDULE?

To fully implement the best practices, non-negotiables should include:

- A least ninety minutes of reading
- Dedicated time for phonics, and whole-class and small-group instruction within the reading block
- Dedicated writing time in addition to reading
- Sixty minutes of math
- Math and reading blocks at the same time across a grade level
- Reading and math blocks staggered throughout the day
- Thirty minutes of intervention every day
- Intervention staggered throughout the day
- Common planning time

For added measure, beyond academic shifts #1, #2, and #3, great schedules might also include:

- Dedicated time for SEL instruction, perhaps as part of the special rotation or morning meeting
- Equitable specials (art, music, PE, etc.) in each school
- All specialists having full teaching loads

horseshoes to golf. In horseshoes, you win by getting the horseshoe close to the pin, and in golf, you only win by getting the ball in the hole.

A real-life story will help bring the analogy to life. One midsized district was deeply committed to providing reading intervention to all struggling readers in its four middle schools. It knew that many sixth graders struggled to read, but historically the middle schools didn't offer classes in reading for these students. A visionary superintendent issued a simple directive: "If we've got kids who can't read and comprehend well, we should teach them to read and comprehend well." This seemed straightforward and logical. Few pushed back, until the middle schools started to build their schedules for the next year. At a senior leadership meeting in late spring, the four principals presented their completed schedules.

PRINCIPAL SCHOOL 1: Obviously, we don't have enough certified staff to teach all the students who struggle to read, but that's okay because we have so many kids below proficiency, it would be way too disruptive to change so many schedules. We are targeting the neediest 10 percent of our students.

SUPERINTENDENT: How many kids are below proficiency in reading?

PRINCIPAL SCHOOL 1: I'm not exactly sure, about 30 percent.

SUPERINTENDENT: I am sure it's 48.5 percent, and you are not helping nearly 80 percent of them. That's not acceptable.

PRINCIPAL SCHOOL 2: (*with a bit of joy or relief in his voice*) We have scheduled 100 percent of our struggling readers for extra help in reading.

SUPERINTENDENT: Wonderful. Who will be teaching these classes and when do they take place?

PRINCIPAL SCHOOL 2: The English teachers will do it during English class.

SUPERINTENDENT: Hold it, that's not extra time, and they are not trained experts in teaching reading.

PRINCIPAL SCHOOL 3: (*with much joy and swagger*) I'm pleased to say that all of our kids are getting extra time to master reading.

SUPERINTENDENT: Great. Same questions, who teaches and when?

PRINCIPAL SCHOOL 3: Title I paraprofessionals will work with our struggling readers. Obviously, there is nothing we can do about students with IEPs, so they aren't part of this. They were already scheduled into a resource room, so we excluded them.

At this point, the superintendent shifted from calm questioning to that of a deeply disappointed, almost dejected leader. "How can this be? We spent a year researching, discussing, and partnering with consultants to rethink how to better serve our struggling students. We are not meeting the needs of many, and we all committed to focusing on reading as the gateway to future learning. We set as a nonnegotiable that all kids in need, 100 percent of struggling readers, would get extra time to learn to read from certified and skilled teachers of reading. We are leaving so many kids behind."

At this point, the three principals, each offended at the reproach, clamored to reiterate their commitment to the concepts espoused but pointed out that the schedule just doesn't allow for such an aspirational goal to become reality. It seems that this vision was just impossible to schedule. Chalk it up to one more pie-in-the-sky central office plan that fell apart once the cold realities of managing a school took over.

But was it impossible? Three good, smart, caring principals said so and definitely believed so. Turning to Principal School 4, the superintendent asked, "I assume you couldn't schedule this either?"

Principal School 4 answered,

Well, at first, we hit all the same walls. We didn't have enough staff to serve all the kids who needed help. The IEPs didn't allow for the new services, and we didn't have time in the day to do both the old services and the new ones. Also the staff were up in arms about kids who struggled to read missing out on a world language or an elective. We landed in a place similar to the other schools.

Very quietly, looking down, the principal continued,

I was really disappointed how far from the mark we ended, and schedules were due to be shared with teachers and kids. We were out of time. I shared my discouragement with the school-based leadership team, and collectively we decided we had to do better. I shared with the community that schedules weren't ready per the plan. We gave ourselves an extra month to figure this out.

After two weeks, we were no better off, so instead of trying to build a schedule around what we had, we asked a very different question. What needed to be in place so we could build the schedule we wanted and kids deserved? We needed to rewrite most of the IEPs, with parental consent; we needed to reduce a few paras through attrition, and scale back on foreign language teachers, and exchange one special educator, and hire four reading teachers with the funds freed up. And so we did. Of course, I met with the staff and explained the shifts and the reasons why. Turns out, it was possible, just hard.

Rather than stopping close to the pin, one school kept trying until it got the ball in the hole.

How to find the time for extra instructional time

Not pulling kids from core instruction (shift #1) is a logistical challenge. Providing extra time to learn (shift #2) is a philosophical challenge as well as a technical one. At first blush, teachers, principals, and central office leaders seem to readily grasp and embrace these ideas. Kids who are academically behind need extra time to fill in the past skill gaps, to be retaught, pre-taught, untaught, and taught differently by a content-strong teacher (shift #3). There is much to cover in just one period a day, so finding extra time for intervention makes sense.

The excitement wanes fast when it comes to actually adding this crucial, life-changing extra-help strategy to the schedule. In my experience, more than half the schools I have worked with bail or water down the effort to the point of limited value. Philosophical arguments, not technical challenges, get in the way.

At the core of the challenge is the simple fact that few existing schedules have big blocks of empty time just waiting for something new to be added. Moreover, few content-strong teachers are sitting around in empty rooms waiting for new intervention classes to be added. It's impossible to add extra time to learn from content-strong teachers without trimming something and some departments. Hard trade-offs need to be made.

The first obstacle is what to reduce to add intervention time. I think push-in and co-teaching have strong followings, in part, because these intervention strategies don't require answering the politically charged question of what to reduce. They happen during already scheduled time, so no change in schedule is needed.

At the elementary level, integrating, rather than cutting, can be a smooth path forward. Adding daily intervention blocks to a schedule than didn't already have one means reducing something. Oddly, lots of folks mistakenly assume that struggling readers might have to miss art, music, PE, or recess. This seems like a bad idea given the importance of educating the whole child and engaging students in school. A better solution is integrating social studies into the reading and writing blocks.

The traditional elementary social studies block typically includes a teacher reading aloud a book tied to the state standards, students reading about historic events tied to the state standards, and students writing and reflecting on what they heard and read. This sounds a lot like the reading and writing block, but all the material is connected to the social studies curriculum. In an integrated approach rather than a separate social studies block, about half of the leveled independent reading books, book reports, read-alouds, and writing assignments are connected to the state social studies standards.

Building extra time into high school schedules to catch up in math, ELA, or reading is a little easier, because all students, whether they struggle or not, already have unique schedules. The common obstacles at this level are tradition, IEPs, and staffing.

When high schools try to wedge an extra period of math, English, or reading into the ninth- or tenth-grade schedule, department turf battles can surface quickly. Everyone seems happy to add the extra instructional time for intervention, but no one wants to give up a period. The science department says science is critical and tested by the state. The world language department touts the benefits of being a world citizen, and so on. A path out of this tug of war is to look at the existing schedules of struggling students. Often, depending on the state's graduation requirements, struggling students as seniors don't take a fourth year of science or social studies. In these cases, schools can add the extra intervention in the freshman year, for example, by delaying, but not eliminating, science or social studies for a year. Improving a student's math skills will make the subsequent years of science more successful, as better writing and comprehension skills will improve future learning in social studies. The wait helps improve, not undermine, the delayed subject.

In some high schools, lots of kids already have extra time in their schedule, but of the wrong kind. Many students with IEPs are scheduled into a resource room with a special education teacher. As noted in prior chapters, this is typically homework help or generalized support, not direct instruction from a content-strong teacher. The simple solution is to rewrite the IEP to include the second period of math or English instead of the resource room. Sometimes the special education team pushes back, but the needed time in the schedule is in plain sight.

Scheduling extra-time intervention at the high school level can also often stumble because there aren't enough content-strong teachers to teach these classes. Absent a great teacher, an extra hour a day of instruction isn't very beneficial. The question is, do you build the schedule with the staff you have or do you staff for the schedule you want (and kids need)? Too often, it's the former. Maybe the math department can squeeze in two intervention periods, and English can wedge in one with the current staff. Unfortunately, this leaves lots of kids unserved and doomed to fall further behind.

From a financial point of view, staffing lots of content-strong interventionists doesn't cost a penny more than current spending. For every intervention period kids have, there is one less period of something else they don't have. It's a case of shifting FTE, not adding FTE. The path forward that is good for kids and good for staff is to build up the number of math, English, and reading teachers through attrition in the other departments that need fewer staff due to fewer students taking these classes. No one loses their job, and all kids get the extra help they need. Two things high schools can also do to ease sliding extra time into the schedule is to make sure intervention classes earn credits and that district graduation requirements don't make it harder to delay a core course or two.

I left the middle school level for last, because it is often the toughest one in which to make the best practices a reality. Many middle schools value grade-level teacher teams, kids having similar experiences, and heterogeneous groupings. These are all things worth valuing, but like everything worth valuing, they may need moderation and balance.

Both middle schools and high schools want their students to succeed. Both can commit to identifying students struggling in math, English, or reading, and providing them extra time with a skilled teacher in the subject of greatest need. This is a shared goal. The means to this goal, however, will look different. To schedule this commonsense, but not common practice, plan in middle schools, a little flexibility is needed, but not a full abandonment of traditional middle school practices.

Teaching teams can't all be just four teachers, because more math and English staff are needed to provide the extra intervention periods. Not all student schedules can be the same either, because some kids have different needs. Starting with the non-negotiables and embracing middle school values can lead to better schedules and more learning.

Sometimes, middle schools try to blend best practices and the middle school model in a way that waters down both, to the disadvantage of all. The most common, less than successful approaches include:

- *Intervention for everyone.* For example, all sixth graders get an extra period of English. Unfortunately, not everyone needs extra help in English and seventh and eighth graders struggle, too.
- *Intervention by everyone.* For example, a schoolwide or whole-grade period in which all teachers, including PE, art, and so on, provide extra help. Not everyone is a content-strong teacher, however.
- *Co-teaching in some of the teams.* No extra time to learn is provided.
- *Foreign language for all.* Delaying the start of learning a second language can open up time in the schedule for kids who need extra help in foundational skills.

Too important to make optional

One plan for finding extra time that means well, but seldom achieves well, is the before- or after-school option. It's an easy, don't rock the boat solution, adding without having to subtract or delay. Unfortunately, this approach, outside the regular day, tells teachers and students alike that it's not that important and it's okay if some kids don't get it due to lack of transportation or other commitments. A better variation on this theme is to offer the missed elective or delayed course before or after school, and the intervention during the day.

Scheduling expertise helps

Building great schedules starts with a clear definition, that is, clarity around the non-negotiables. The story of the four middle school principals earlier in the chapter highlighted the power of knowing when it's okay to declare the schedule done and done well. It also highlighted the importance of scheduling expertise. All four principals wanted to provide struggling students extra time to master reading taught by a skilled teacher of reading, but not all knew how to actually do it.

NEWS FLASH! Not all principals or assistant principals or guidance counselors assigned the task of creating the master schedule are, in fact, expert schedulers. They are eager folks doing the best they can, but many have no formal training, and few got the task because of a strong aptitude for building schedules.

One of the four principals did create a schedule that met all the criteria; three wanted to but couldn't. What happened next is telling. The superintendent directed the three schools that had less than excellent schedules to revise their schedules to meet the non-negotiables. Even with the insights gleaned from their colleague, all three principals reported back at the next senior leadership meeting that in their schools, it just wasn't possible. At this point, the superintendent did something I had never seen before. He tasked Principal School 4 to build the schedules for the other three schools. All four principals hated the idea, but if they couldn't meet the requirements, then someone else would.

Through an uneasy alliance, Principal School 4 helped his colleagues build great schedules. As a bonus, because he built the schedules for all the schools, he added a gift to each. All the reading teachers in all four schools would have their prep period before lunch, have lunch at the same time, and then have professional learning community (PLC) time after lunch. This created a two-hour block of time when every reading teacher in all the schools was free from instructional responsibilities. This common window across the four schools encouraged the reading teachers to gather together once a week to plan, eat, bond, and support each other. They rotated the meeting from school to school each week.

Beyond building great schedules, reading scores jumped, and over time, achievement in all subjects improved, dropout rates plunged 64 percent, and the superintendent was honored at the White House by President Obama. It seems the first step to the presidential rose garden is a great schedule.

Scheduling is a team sport

Why do so few people profess love and affection for the schedules they build? It's not just that the schedules are hard to build and full of tough trade-offs. One reason is that after hours of toiling to do the best they can juggling a myriad of trade-offs, school schedules often come up short of the desired best practices. Speech therapists don't want to pull kids from math, reading teachers don't want to group kids with different needs, and no one feels good about providing content-strong interventions to just half the students who need it. It's hard to love the schedules many schools have, but it's harder yet to figure out how to build a better schedule. Expertise helps, but so does scheduling as a team.

Effective scheduling, to the surprise of many, is actually a team sport, not an individual undertaking. When I speak to school and district leaders about building a schedule, the image that fills their heads is a school leader sitting alone in front of a computer screen full of colored blocks wrestling with an endless series of trade-offs. Maybe it's a picture of a frustrated and bewildered administrator copying and pasting last year's schedule into software or Excel and tweaking it to reflect next year's staffing and priorities.

Here is an image that seldom comes to mind: the entire senior leadership team at both the school and district levels on a trust-building ropes course, or all the teachers in a school at an Amish barn raising. At a ropes course, everyone has to work together to get across the high wire and over the wall. No matter how strong, agile, or independent you are, the team can't succeed unless everyone works together. Often the strong must help the less athletic, and everyone has something to contribute. An Amish barn is built quickly and well, because so many help. These are team efforts, and so is great schedule building.

Implementing the shifts to 100 percent core instruction, extra time to learn, content-strong instruction, and prevention-focused SEB supports just isn't possible without building lots of great schedules. And that takes teamwork. In practice, this means creating scheduling parties where all the needed folks are in the room. Pizza helps, too. Who needs to be invited to the scheduling party?

ELEMENTARY PRINCIPALS AND CLASSROOM TEACHERS. Too often, an inspired principal takes the schedule home over a weekend and toils to build a great schedule. The schedule clearly defines when reading will be taught and math and everything else, so others know when they can and can't pull out students. Remember, kids who struggle need extra help, but they also need 100 percent of core instruction. If a special educator or speech therapist doesn't know when Latisha's class is being taught reading, how can they schedule pullout with certainty that they won't undermine core instruction?

The principal also ensures that each grade (or even adjacent grades) has similar schedules so that students can be grouped across classrooms who have similar needs. This also facilitates common planning time. The schedule includes SEL instruction as part of the specials rotation, has daily grade-level intervention blocks, and lastly and most controversially, it staggers reading and math blocks throughout the day. The principal correctly reasoned that if everyone taught reading first thing in the morning, say from 8:30 to 10:00, then either speech, PT, OT, and special education pullout would be blocked from working with any student during this entire window (100 percent of core is a nonnegotiable) or kids would miss some core instruction to get other supports. Staggering reading and math throughout the day balances everyone's needs. Or does it?

When the principal shared the well-designed schedule with the classroom teachers, anger, not praise flowed. No one liked teaching reading in the afternoon, others didn't like when math was assigned, and some grade-level teams wanted different schedules from their peers. Many wanted to move this block or that and didn't appreciate being told that they couldn't.

The principal had wrestled with the trade-offs, but the teachers hadn't. They were presented with a finished product without wrangling with the many constraints and goals. A better solution for principals is to partner with classroom teachers and build the schedule together, in real time, all in the same room, with the schedule template projected onto a screen. Sometimes each grade sends just one representative, but it's a collective effort either way.

One such principal, burned by working solo, shifted to a more collaborative approach to scheduling. The whole school would build the elementary master schedule during a faculty meeting. The principal started the session by building understanding and clarity on the non-negotiables. When the staggered reading blocks were placed in the schedule, teachers from grades 4 and 5 objected, in the moment. "We want to teach reading in the morning," they explained. Here, the principal pointed out that if they do, speech, OT, PT, and others will have no choice but to pull kids out of reading and math in order to meet the IEPs. If reading is staggered, he explained, then no one gets pulled from reading. "Oh, that's why you did that staggering. I thought you just didn't realize that it's better to teach reading in the morning," explained one teacher. Another added, "We definitely don't want kids pulled from reading." Happily, the second-grade team offered to take an afternoon reading block, so that the fourth grade could move to the morning. All was well for teachers and kids.

The point is that when principals shield staff from the hard decisions of scheduling, it makes it easier for them to push back on the final product. Collaboratively building schedules builds buy-in and better schedules.

In one Midwestern district, twenty-one elementary principals embraced collaborative scheduling with remarkable results:

- Ninety-three percent gained agreement with staff on top priorities and non-negotiables.
- Eighty-one percent created clear guidelines for when support staff could push in or pull out, up from 0 percent.
- Seventy-five percent held scheduling parties so all interrelated staff schedules could be built at the same time.

All schools reported a more collaborative, less stressful process that allowed them to provide more and better intervention and protect core instruction.

ELEMENTARY CLASSROOM TEACHERS AND SPECIAL EDUCATION, RELATED SERVICES, AND INTERVENTION STAFF. One of the primary goals of involving classroom teachers in building the master schedule is too ensure that the final plan supports the three academic shifts, ensuring that special education staff and interventionists like reading teachers can push in, pull out, and intervene at the right times.

Unfortunately, even the most thoughtful master schedule is useless if folks don't stick to it. This is what I call the *carpool conundrum*. Imagine Mrs. Jones, a caring, thoughtful teacher, driving to work by herself. She is a bit early, so she decides to stop for coffee. The line is long, but no problem, she will be on time.

But let's rewrite the scene. Mrs. Jones is carpooling with two colleagues, Mr. Washington and Ms. Garcia. One has a before-school parent meeting, and the other needs to finish grading a few papers before the opening bell rings. Still, Mrs. Jones is ahead of schedule, although her car mates are not. Being a caring colleague, Mrs. Jones skips the pit stop for coffee because she doesn't want to make Mr. Washington late for his meeting or stress out Ms. Garcia.

When driving to work, it is obvious whether you are carpooling or commuting alone. It's less obvious to many classroom teachers that they are in a figurative carpool with special educators, related services, and general education interventionists like reading teachers. If classroom teachers don't stick with the master schedule and teach reading and math as planned, then a speech therapist can't be sure he or she isn't inadvertently pulling a student from math or reading.

PRINCIPALS WHO SHARE STAFF. The frustration can be palpable. A principal is close to achieving the perfect schedule. However, Mary, the art teacher, is needed on Tuesday morning, but she doesn't come until Tuesday afternoon. This upends the specials rotation and quickly leads to the loss of common planning time and daily intervention in grades four and five. If only Mary could come in the morning.

She can't because the principal of Mary's other school has completed her schedule, and it's unreasonable to ask her to scrap it and start again. If the two principals had been in the same room, building their schedules together, Mary very likely could have been scheduled differently, great for one school and just fine for the other.

SPECIAL EDUCATION, RELATED SERVICES, AND INTERVENTION STAFF. All these folks are jostling to serve many of the same students. If they all build their schedules at the same time, all in the same room, then they can better coordinate building groups of students with similar needs and respect the no-pullout times.

PRINCIPALS AND CENTRAL OFFICE LEADERS. In most districts, principals or site-based teams build the schedules for their schools. This seems to please everyone. The principals appreciate the autonomy, and the central office is plenty busy without a new task on its plate. Unfortunately, the best practices for struggling students and the required shifts in practice often fall victim to this division of labor. While principals reasonably want a say in their school's schedule, they often lack the authority to make all the needed adjustments to implement the best practices.

This takes us back to horseshoes, rather than golf. Many principals build the best schedules they can, but that's not the same as building the best schedules.

When principals or other site-based schedule builders say things like the following, it's time to cooperate more closely with central office:

- Some IEPs are written in ways that don't allow us to schedule intervention well.
- I wish we didn't have to provide _____ for every student. It's not the best use of time.
- I wish I had more _____ staff. I could live with a bit less of _____.
- I wish _____ worked in the school on a different day or time.
- Why do we still do _____? I don't think it makes sense anymore.

In many of these cases, a principal doesn't have the authority to resolve the situation, but the head of special education, teaching and learning, or HR can.

·················

Scheduling isn't exciting; it's not flashy and seldom fun. It is, however, key to effectively implementing the shifts in practice that will best prepare students for success in life. By starting with unambiguous non-negotiables, infusing expertise, and making scheduling a team sport, this annual task can become a strategic lever for good. Like the Amish barn raising, when the whole community works together, many hands lighten the hard work and all benefit.

CHAPTER 8

Shift #6: From Managing Compliance to Managing Practice, Too

IN THE FIRST FIVE SHIFTS, teachers change their practice, schools change their schedules, and teams change IEPs. It should be no surprise then that leaders and managers also have to change. What might be surprising is that the very definition of an effective leader must change, along with sweeping revisions to roles, responsibilities, and the organizational chart.

Many districts have a leadership paradox. Special educators, school psychologists, reading teachers, interventionists, and others who help struggling students have among the most complex, difficult, wide-ranging jobs, but get less help than other teachers in a typical school system. They build their own schedules, but other don't. They devise interventions and academic services with less direction from teaching and learning experts. They are asked to assess eligibility and complete lengthy IEP documents but are seldom coached on how to do this well, quickly, and constantly.

Yes, managers and leaders help, but often they step in at moments of crisis or with irate parents. They jump into action if compliance rates drop, but they provide much less guidance on how to improve teacher craft and day-to-day work. These leaders are firefighters, rather than guides and coaches.

A comparison of elementary classroom teachers with their special education peers is telling. In one typical school I visited, classroom teachers received instructional coaching a few times a week; had weekly principal walk-throughs; got feedback on classroom management, student engagement, and pedagogy; planned with colleagues every day; and attended monthly faculty meetings focused primarily on peers sharing best teaching practices. In the same school, special educators received no instructional coaching, no supervisor walks-throughs, and no common planning time, and faculty meetings never addressed special education–related topics.

Special educators also receive far less support and guidance on how to use their precious time than general educators. Classroom teachers are given schedules, pacing guides, and detailed reading block recommendations, such as twenty minutes of phonics, forty minutes of small-group instructions, ten minutes of vocabulary, and so on. Special educators, school psychologists, and related service providers are simply instructed to "meet the IEP minutes" and stay within the compliance time lines. They are left to figure all this out on their own. Unlike general educators, in most districts, no one helps special education or intervention staff allocate their time. How much time is allotted for meetings? For working with students? For counseling?

Additionally, while general education teachers don't decide how many kids will be in the classroom, special educators and reading teachers, for example, are left to set the size of their own groups. The unspoken directive is "just get it done and meet all the IEP requirements."

A twenty-year veteran classroom teacher might receive fifty times more guidance than a second-year special educator. To be fair, there are no villains in these situations, only victims. Special education directors are spread too thin, principals don't have the needed expertise or time, and special educators do so many different things that it would be hard to imagine what exactly any coaching would focus on. The "leave them alone except when there is a problem" system of management is so common because incredibly dedicated staff make it work, but this adds great pressure to an already demanding job.

When I was a superintendent, I managed special education differently from everything else. My leadership team will say I was a bit controlling and detailed. I knew room by room how many kids where in a class, I reviewed schedules to ensure every high school teacher or elementary specialist had a full teaching load, and I insisted the instructional coaches share their weekly schedule and that PLC teams report on what they focused on each month. It wasn't that I didn't trust people, but I considered their time and talent a precious resource that deserved collective oversight, planning, and managing. That said, I didn't know how any special educator used his or her time or grouped kids, or if they were overloaded or underutilized.

WHAT'S A LEADER OR MANAGER TO DO?

The hands-off approach to day-to-day management and leadership doesn't help kids or teachers. It contributes to staff burnout and will make implementing the six shifts much more difficult. Effective managers and leaders in the twenty-first century must actively support the first five shifts. This includes both tactical and strategic efforts. On the tactical side:

- *Help guide staff on how they use their time.* While there is no one right way for special education and intervention staff to use their time, not setting guidelines and expectations is never best. Provide guidance on how many hours a week they should work with students; how many students to work with, on average; how much time to allocate to assessing eligibility; and so on. These guidelines change role to role, may be different in elementary versus secondary schools, and will have some exceptions. Such guidelines are best developed in partnership with staff. The impact on services to students can be huge. One district reviewed how its precious reading teachers used their time. No one thought there was a problem, but no had really thought about it. The reading teachers and district leaders met a few times to wrestle with questions such as how many sessions were a reasonable day's work and what was the optimal group size (assuming groups were of students with similar needs). The consensus was eight groups a day, not the current average of five, and five students instead of four. It seemed reasonable to staff and doable if they were excused from a few meetings that they thought they didn't need to attend, and it also doubled the number of students getting expert help from talented reading teachers. (See figure 8.1 for a visualization.)

- *Help staff build their schedules.* Once guidelines are set on how best to use time, schedules convert aspirations into reality. Not every special educator or interventionist is a great scheduler, and even if they are, their schedule highly depends on other schedules. Managers need to help coordinate and align many peoples' schedules so that they reflect the use of time priorities established.
- *Help streamline meetings and paperwork.* More than half of all special education and intervention staff time is devoted to meetings and paperwork. Roughly $75 billion a year is devoted to these activities. Since it represents half of any district's special education spending, it's not unreasonable that managers help improve the efficiency of completing these needed tasks.

FIGURE 8.1
Setting guidelines for reading teachers

GROUPS TAUGHT PER DAY

AVERAGE STUDENT GROUP SIZE		5	6	7	8	9
	4	20	24	28	32	36
	5	25	30	35	40	45
	5	30	36	42	48	54

The number of students served per reading teacher increased from 20 to 40. The 8 groups a day equaled 4 hours of instruction, about 90 minutes less than a typical classroom teacher.

- *Share best practices to guide what's written into an IEP.* The law is clear: the IEP team knows what's best for each student. That said, why are we so confident that everyone around the table is fluent in best practices? Reviews of hundreds of thousands of IEPs says it's not always the case.

Managing supports for struggling students involves a lot of logistics, and managers need to help smooth these out, but that's not enough. They need to also lead by shaping vision, instilling values, and ultimately improving outcomes. The more strategic role of leaders and managers should:

- *Identify current and needed staff strengths.* Gone are the days when leaders and managers could think of their staff as interchangeable superheroes. Managers should help identify who is strong at what, creating building assignments that ensure the needed mix of strengths in each school, and hire to fill any gaps in areas of specialization.
- *Provide coaching and guidance to improve teacher craft.* Managers and leaders should help their staff get better at what they do. It seems so basic, yet it's not very common for special educators. Most direction provided is on updates to state laws or reporting requirements or new IEP software. Receiving help on working directly with students is much less common.
- *Elevate the importance of outcomes to be equal with compliance.* Shift the focus to results and provide meaningful data on what's working for kids and what's not. If leaders talk and intervene mostly when compliance rules change or noncompliance erupts, they signal to staff that this is the most important aspect of their jobs. What gets talked about get valued. What gets measured, gets managed.
- *View success through the lens of equity.* All leaders need to lead the charge for greater equity of access and outcomes. Special education and intervention are no exception. A particular area

of focus is rethinking the relationship between race and special education. Students of color are overidentified as having a disability in many districts, expectations are lower in some, and providing help and comfort sometimes replaces scaffolding, high expectations, and great outcomes.

- *Help foster a focus on prevention.* Foster the culture and systems that prevent student outbursts and intervene early so that students don't needed added services.

NEW ROLES REQUIRE NEW SKILLS

If leaders and managers reading this list are overwhelmed, I can understand. It is a lot more than what's on already-full plates. But remember that special educators and interventionists are tasked with doing all this on their own, on top of a full caseload. So, how can leaders and managers do all that's needed?

The first step in shifting from managing compliance to managing practice, too, is to value and seek a different kind of expertise in managers and leaders. Most special educator leaders are experts in "special education." To be honest, I'm not totally sure what it means to be an expert in special education, but a close approximation might be knowing a lot about compliance, interacting with parents, hiring general-purpose staff, and allocating staff to schools. Many are not, and couldn't reasonably be expected to be, expertise in everything that their staff do. Could one person be an expert in speech therapy, autism, teaching reading, streamlining meetings, behavior management, budgeting, assessing student growth and program effectiveness, math, scheduling, assessing student eligibility, mental health counseling, and of course compliance?

In districts that have fewer than ten thousand students, one or two generalists typically oversee everyone in the special education department. The special ed director might have been a speech pathologist, but hires and supervises all special educators, school psychologists, occupational therapists, staff for behavior and autism programs, and more. I've worked with many dedicated special education directors who were top-notch school psychologists who readily admit in private they have no background or training in teaching and learning best practices, budgeting, or autism. Despite this, they manage all that and more.

Larger districts have a semblance of specialization based on expertise, but often it too is overly broad. For example, there may be a director of substantially separate programs, but this encompasses autism, behavior, and cognitive impairment. The director typically has expertise in one but not all three areas. Similarly, the director of related services would likely have been a speech therapist, but the hiring process seldom focused on their ability to build schedules or streamline meetings and paperwork. Sadly, even in the largest districts, too few in special education leadership self-report deep expertise in teaching and learning best practices. This is changing, but slowly. They, like their staff, are asked to do it all regardless of skill, training, interest, or aptitude. It's no wonder that the candidate pool for special education directors is so thin. The job is very tough, given the incredible range of functions and roles they oversee.

When pressed on this seemingly overwhelming job, some folks suggest that the building principals pick up some of the load as the instructional leaders in the school and managers of special education staff in their building. Interviews with thousands of staff and principals suggest otherwise. Principals also report not having the needed expertise to provide most of the tactical support needed, and many lack the bandwidth to provide the more strategic help.

The comparison to general education leadership is stark. Directors of teaching and learning are well versed in best practices in teaching and learning and are aided by a team with specialized expertise. For example, math department heads are expert at teaching math, instructional technology leaders have deep experience in utilizing tech, and lead reading teachers are experts at teaching reading. None of these folks are asked to lead outside their area of expertise. Not surprisingly, content department heads and heads of teaching and learning are highly sought-after positions with very low turnover. Often only retirement or promotion, but seldom burnout, leads to a vacancy.

TEAMWORK CAN PROVIDE EXPERTISE

Given the complex task of leading and managing special education, intervention, and SEB services, a team of experts to implement the six shifts is needed. No one person can do it all. They need expertise in the following areas (see table 8.1). The following list can help leaders form a well-rounded leadership team:

DOMAINS EXPERTISE
- Teaching reading
- Teaching and learning best practices
- Prevention-based behavior management
- Mental health services
- Speech and language, occupational therapy, and physical therapy
- Students with autism
- Students with intellectual disability
- Compliance

SKILL EXPERTISE
- Setting guidelines for use of time and group size
- Scheduling
- Budgeting
- Hiring based on skill set
- Program evaluation
- Giving constructive and actionable feedback to teachers on their craft
- Streamlining meetings and paperwork
- Managing external partnership

TABLE 8.1

Is your leadership and management structure well suited to raise achievement for struggling students, reduce staff burnout, and manage costs?

	WHO CURRENTLY LEADS AND MANAGES		HAS REQUIRED EXPERTISE?	HAS SUFFICIENT TIME?	SCORE
Domains expertise	**General education**	**Special education**	**(Yes, sort of, no)**	**(Yes, sort of, no)**	
Teaching reading					
Teaching and learning best practices					
Prevention-based behavior management					
Mental health services					
Speech and language, occupational therapy, and physical therapy					
Students with autism					
Students with intellectual disability					
Compliance					
Skill expertise					
Setting guidelines for use of time and group size					
Scheduling					
Budgeting					
Hiring based on skill set					
Program evaluation					
Give constructive and actionable feedback to teachers on their craft					
Streamlining meetings and paperwork					
Managing external partnership					

(continues)

TABLE 8.1 *Continued*

| Leadership expertise | WHO CURRENTLY LEADS AND MANAGES | | HAS REQUIRED EXPERTISE? | HAS SUFFICIENT TIME? | SCORE |
	General education	Special education	(Yes, sort of, no)	(Yes, sort of, no)	
Setting a vision of high expectations and an outcomes orientation					
Championing equity					
Motivating staff in a high-stress environment					

HOW TO SCORE

Points for coherence: Give yourself 1 point for every row where the same person leads the effort for both general education and general education students

Points for gaps: Take a point away for if you couldn't name or agree on who leads and manages for either general education or special education

Points for expertise: 1 point if you answer yes, 0 points for sort of, and take a point away for no.

Points for sufficient time: 1 point if you answer yes, 0 points for sort of, and take a point away for no.

HOW DID YOU DO?

If you score was:

Over 40 points	On the right track
26–39 points	Getting close, but still room to grow
1–25 points	A few pieces are in place
0 points or less	Not ready to implement the 6 shifts. Don't feel bad; you have a lot of company

LEADERSHIP EXPERTISE

- Setting a vision of high expectations and an outcomes orientation
- Championing equity
- Motivating staff in a high-stress environment

The list is long and diverse, and the tasks are already assigned to current leaders and managers. One person is unlikely to have all this expertise. Any group of ten would be unlikely to have all this expertise.

In smaller districts, a ten-person special education leadership team will seem wildly out of budget. Even in districts with ten thousand students, ten leaders and managers may seem like a lot. The key to affordability is not to think about every area of expertise as being headed by a full-time manager or even a manager at all. It will take distributed leadership, teamwork, and a new definition of who is a manager. Moreover, not all of these leaders need be within the special education department.

In small and midsized districts, teacher leaders can cost-effectively infuse the desired expertise. A speech therapist could be paid a stipend to help his or her colleagues improve their craft. A really efficient school psychologist could be compensated a bit more for helping others streamline the evaluation and IEP writing process and on-boarding new school psychologists in these time-saving practices.

Existing leaders outside special education can also provide much of the needed expertise. The chief academic officer is the logical person to deal with teaching and learning best practices for all students, including students with disabilities or who struggle without an IEP. The business office can player a bigger role in staffing and budgeting and evaluating the effectiveness of special education, and RTI services needn't be part of the special education budget or department.

Looking for the needed leadership skills from a staff who may not even work in the department needing the skill can help cost-effectively round out the leadership team. For example, one district had a behaviorist who happened to be an expert scheduler. She helped over forty special educators, related service professionals, and reading teachers build their schedules each year. Was this in the job description for a behavior specialist? Of course not, but it played to her strengths and interest. She loved the work, appreciated the small stipend, and helped a lot of kids and staff implement student-centered cost-effective schedules. The district spent $3,500, the behaviorist spent about a week over the course of a few weeks, and the district realized it didn't need to fill three vacant positions, which was great because it couldn't find qualified candidates.

Certainly, special education leaders, SEB directors, and other full-time managers will still provide a great deal of direction. Hopefully, if others meet many of the technical and domain needs, the people at the top can concentrate on the strategic areas of expertise including setting a vision, motivating staff, improving equity, and shifting the focus to outcomes as well as compliance.

The larger the district, the easier it is to afford dedicated staff with the needed expertise, but the mind-set of being good at special education undermines expertise-based leadership even in very large districts. In one district with more than forty thousand students, for example, the leadership team was smart, caring, and hardworking. It also didn't match skills to role. For example, the head of related services was a former occupational therapist. Her ability to help the fifty-plus speech therapists become better speech therapists was limited. It is sad that so many people never receive coaching to hone their craft. The director of substantially separate programs oversaw more than two hundred substantially separate classrooms serving students with autism, behavior, and intellectual disabilities. She was quite skilled in behavior management, but not very familiar with best practices in the other two fields. The head of school psychologists was very skilled at the IEP process, evaluation, and compliance, but was also in charge of the behavior support staff because some of these folks were school psychologists. She, however, had no formal training or experience in the domain. Lastly, the dedicated director of special education was working hard to deeply understand academic best practices, but had no formal training in this, as she had come up the school psychologist ranks.

Every one of these leaders and managers worked really hard and learned much about all the corners of the departments they led, but it was stressful and an awful lot of learning on the job. Few math department heads, by contrast, don't bring to the job deep expertise in teaching math on their first day.

A NEW ORGANIZATIONAL CHART FOR A NEW ERA

Creating a management and leadership team that prizes distributed leadership and expertise doesn't fit neatly into the typical organizational chart. The org chart of the future will look different. It will prioritize leaders with role-specific expertise, be more cross-functional, and will include more teacher leaders as well.

One key difference will likely be the centralization of the leadership of all academics under one person rather than a split between general education, Title I, and special education leaders. Most districts proclaim, "They are all our students," followed by a passionate phrase, "And *all* means *all*." While sincere in thought, the org chart typically reinforces separation, not unity. The teaching and learning team should oversee all things teaching and learning. This includes developing, sharing, training, and managing the implementation of best practices for core instruction, intervention, and special education academic support. To make this a reality, the team must also have meaningful input into what academic supports are written into IEPs.

In midsized or larger districts, say five thousand students or more, there should be a districtwide director of reading within the teaching and learning department. Reading is simply too important not to have expert dedicated leadership. For urban districts of this size, a director of secondary reading is also a must-have if all kids are going to be college- and career-ready upon graduation.

Tomorrow, like today, the special education department will remain the primary leader for identifying and evaluating students with disabilities and writing IEPs. While this won't change, a few aspects might. Having a centralized evaluation team that is district based, not school based, for initial evaluations can bring consistency to a highly variable process. The teaching and learning team will find it easier to partner with the initial IEP writing team to embed best-practice supports into the IEPs. The centralized initial evaluation team can also spring into action every time a student with an IEP moves into the district. It doesn't seem fair that if a district embraces best practices for raising achievement, kids new to the district should be anchored by an IEP that was written elsewhere and may not be at the forefront of what works.

Helping students with more severe needs deserves dedicated leadership as well. The leadership team needs expertise in programming for students with autism, severe behaviors, and intellectual disabilities. Seldom will one person be highly knowledgeable in all three. Teacher leaders can bridge the knowledge gap in smaller districts that can't afford (or need) full-time leaders. Similarly, each of the related services deserves leadership with expertise, but again, often through teacher leaders.

Behavior management and counseling deserves its own home in nearly every district. Since more than half the students typically receiving these services don't have IEPs, there is no reason that this function is part of special education. Staff specialization helps make moving this function much easier. If some school psychologists focus on IEP development, eligibility determination, and case management, and others focus on behavior or counseling, it will be clear which department each belongs to. If school psychologists remain Jacks and Jills of all trades, then this specialized leadership becomes unmanageable.

Creating the much-needed department of counseling and behavior supports will also force, in a good way, clarification of the often overly broad commitment to SEL. As mentioned earlier, SEL means a hundred different things to fifty different people. Separating SEL into three broad elements—(1) social emotional competencies like compassion, grit, empathy, and collaboration, (2) mental health, and (3) problematic behavior—can help create a more effective leadership structure and, in turn, more effective implementation of all three important SEL goals. While the last two belong in the unified behavior management and counseling department, the first does not.

Teaching SEL competencies is a teaching task, not a support service. It is a discrete set of skills to be taught, and it should be interwoven with teaching content. It deserves dedicated time in the schedule, and it competes with other academic demands on the schedule. For all these reasons, it best belongs in the teaching and learning department. If we believe, as most do today, that developing grit or empathy matters as much as math or history, they should be treated as equals within the teaching and learning function, rather than as a stepchild, outside the family circle.

For districts pursuing strategies of building extensive community-based partnerships, this responsibility and some dedicated staff would also be part of the behavior and counseling department. In addition, expertise in scheduling and streamlining meetings and paperwork should be somewhere in the organization. Neither one is a full-time job and neither requires a specific certification or title, but it should be designated, valued, and compensated.

Finally, someone in the central office should also be tasked with managing, scheduling, and training paraprofessionals districtwide. If a district spends over a million dollars a year on paraprofessionals, roughly forty or fifty folks, a full-time manager would be a great investment. Anything less than a half-time manager might be penny wise and pound foolish.

The org chart of the future will have three branches (1) teaching and learning, (2) special education, and (3) behavior and mental health, as detailed in figures 8.2, 8.3, and 8.4.

A shift to an expertise-based, distributed, and collaborative leadership structure can be confusing for school-based staff and building principals. Clarifying and rethinking decision-making rights can smooth implementation of the new org chart; failing to do so often leads to turf battles or disjointed, ineffective implementation. Being clear about who makes which decision is crucial. The typical org chart with boxes, lines, and dashed lines doesn't really detail who has ultimate authority to make a decision or give input before a decision is made. Clarity is a must, especially for principals.

FIGURE 8.2

Teaching and learning organizational chart

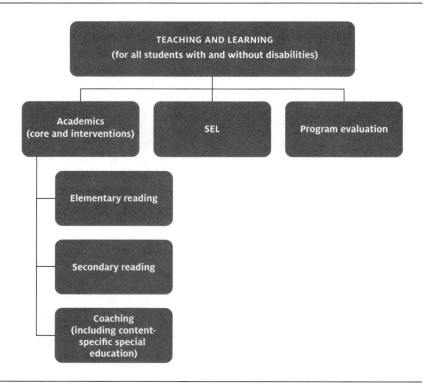

School principals are central to the effective implementation of the six shifts. If decisions are made without them, they will have difficulty championing the efforts. Thus, principals need to have greater voice, understanding, and buy-in when establishing how to serve struggling students with and without disabilities. Districts need to clarify principals' decision-making rights when hiring and evaluating special education, intervention, behavior, and mental health staff who work in their schools. Some schools have adopted the two-yes rule. For example, no special educator can be hired to work in a school without signoff by both the principal and the special educator's supervisor.

Compared to current practice, I suspect this feels like an army of managers, and cries of ballooning bureaucracy might spew from some

FIGURE 8.3

Special education organizational chart

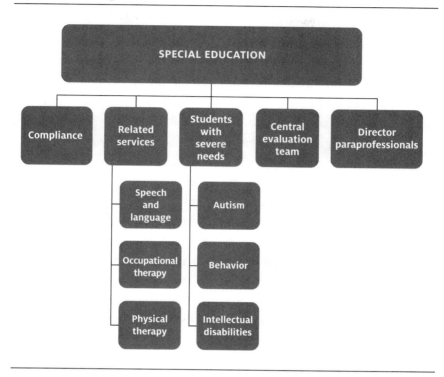

FIGURE 8.4

Behavior and mental health organizational chart

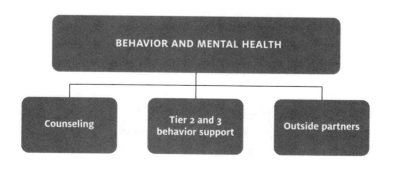

school board members. To anyone who works outside K–12, however, it will feel very normal. To an outsider, what is most surprising about traditional org charts is that some roles don't seem to have anyone managing them at all.

In many hundreds of interviews with paraprofessionals, I often hear that they aren't sure who is their boss. For serious problems, they reach out to the principal or special education director, but on a day-to-day basis, they often receive little or no direction. Some say the classroom teacher is in charge of them, but the very same teacher frequently reports that they think the grade-level special educator oversees the paraprofessional. Sometimes, special educators acknowledge their leadership role, but quickly point out that they have no regular meetings and don't evaluate or try to improve the quality of the paraprofessionals' support. Being in charge often means making sure they are in the right place with the right kids. De facto, they guide the location of their work, not the quality of the work itself.

One district that had many paraprofessionals exemplified the lack of paraprofessional supervision and the benefits of closer supervision. The district had over two hundred special education paraprofessionals; upon review, it was unclear who was in charge of them. The special ed director thought principals managed the paraprofessionals in their buildings, and the principals reported they didn't. "They are in the special education department," they retorted. The paraprofessionals knew the truth: "We really don't get much direction," they shared.

Two hundred and forty staff members without a boss is a big investment going unmanaged. The superintendent decided to appoint a director of paraprofessionals. This seems like a no-brainer, but the school board and some in the superintendent's cabinet thought this a frivolous and unwise expense. The superintendent stated the obvious, but seldom considered facts. How big is a department of 240 paraprofessionals? It's more staff than four elementary schools with a principal in each. It's ten times bigger than the social studies department that had a half-time leader, and it was over $6 million in spending, a big number no matter what the comparison. Undeterred, the superintendent transferred an existing staff member into this new position mid-school year, as a trial.

New to the position, the director of paraprofessionals sought to get a basic understanding of her new world. Who were these 240 folks, what did they do, and how could she help them? The third question was easy to answer. A quick visit to all the schools and lots of conversations revealed hardworking paraprofessionals hungry for role clarification, help with problematic behaviors, requests for basic supplies, and more equitable workloads. The first two questions were a lot harder to answer.

Neither HR nor the special ed department had an up-to-date list of paraprofessionals and their assignments. Staff turnover, students coming and leaving the district, and revised IEPs meant that the list developed just before the start of the school was out of date by October and useless by January.

The new director met with each principal and quickly developed the roster of paraprofessionals in the district, school by school. Figuring out what each paraprofessional did was much more difficult. The principals knew if the paraprofessional was assigned one-on-one to a specific student or to a substantially separate classroom, but that covered far fewer than half of her new charges. It took over forty hours of conversations with school-based special ed staff and the paraprofessionals themselves to get a clear picture of who did what. As a quick reality check, for no other role in the district, let alone one so big and costly, would it take a new leader so long to learn who is in the department and what they are assigned to do.

The director's research was well worth the effort. It revealed a lot, including:

- Roughly twenty FTEs had slid into nonspecial education work, like bus duty, recess, office work, copying, and the like. Often this was just part of their day, not their only role, but the bits and pieces did add up to twenty FTEs in total.
- Seventeen paraprofessionals assigned one-on-one to students had no such students to support. The kids had moved or were

out for a long-term illness. When students with paraprofessional support on their IEP moved into the district, schools always asked for more paraprofessionals, but when kids moved out, they weren't as quick to share the news.

- Many paraprofessionals didn't have full-time work, even though they were full-time staff. For example, when students they supported went to related services or the resource room, they had nothing to do but wait alone. A handful of paraprofessionals who helped kids with mobility or transition issues worked with them between classes but didn't have much to do during class time. They did join their students in class, but the students' need was between classes.

- Most worrisome, many paraprofessionals provided academic support and instruction, despite limited training or skill in teaching the subject.

Another district that conducted such an audit found a few dozen non-English-speaking paraprofessionals, originally hired as ELL paraprofessionals, assigned to help students with academic support for whom English was their first (and only) language.

Over the next few months, the new supervisor reassigned underutilized staff, clawed back their time from nonspecial ed services, and created micro-schedules, parsing out where to be in thirty-minute increments to take advantage of the time their students didn't need paraprofessional support. Over the longer run, she changed the hiring criteria, revised IEPs, and allowed paraprofessionals to specialize a bit as well, opting in or out of working with students with challenging behaviors. There was more than enough work to keep a full-time leader busy, and kids, staff, and the budget all benefited.

The paraprofessional role isn't the only one in the typical organizational structure that gets less support, guidance, and leadership than it deserves. Another somewhat common case of undersupervision is that in many districts, no one actively supervises social workers and mental health counselors on a day-to-day basis. This shortcoming is rooted in the practice of forming departments based on staff title, rather than function.

Usually, school psychologists are in the special education department. They report to a special education supervisor and go to special ed PD, for example. They clearly play on the special ed team. Guidance counselors are equally well organized. They wear team guidance department jerseys. In some districts, social workers and mental health counselors are people without a place to call home. Because they aren't special education–certified, they aren't part of special ed and definitely aren't part of the guidance department because, again, they aren't certified as such. They serve students in both general ed and special ed, and they counsel, but don't do all that guidance counselors do. A surprising number of social workers and mental health counselors share that they feel like a third wheel. One large district with fifty social workers only realized how adrift its mental health staff were when it emailed out the agenda for a districtwide PD day and it hadn't assigned a room or topic to the social workers.

TOO MUCH MANAGEMENT OR NOT ENOUGH?

The recommended leadership structure might seem top-heavy. There are a lot more folks in charge in this plan than in the typical district plan. It's not a love of bureaucracy that drives the design, but the realization that expertise matters and that special education and general education interventions have historically stretched their leaders too thin.

No other sector asks leaders and managers to oversee so many or so much. Walk into a hospital, law firm, engineering office, or other white-collar, knowledge-based organization, and you will find vastly more management and much more focused leadership. In professional service organizations, there is one supervisor for roughly every –eight to fifteen frontline staff. In many districts, forty special educators report to a single director, or seventh-five related service professionals report to one supervisor. In the example of the district that received pushback for investing in a director of paraprofessionals, even after creating the new position, there was only one manager for 240 staff.

Not only do current leaders and managers oversee two or three or even twenty times as many people as other knowledge-based organizations, they oversee a much wider breadth of disciplines. The head of intensive care nursing only oversees intensive care nursing. The manager of structural engineering doesn't oversee mechanical, chemical, and electrical engineering, and something totally outside their skill set like sales. Yet I routinely see a special education leader oversee speech and language, occupational therapy, physical therapy, special ed identification, counseling, state compliance reporting, and out-of-district placements. This would be unthinkable in other sectors.

If a district's question is, "How can we afford so much overhead?" I think the reverse is a better question: "How will you ever shift services to twenty-first-century best practices with overloaded managers and leaders supervising many disparate domains, some of which are by necessity outside their field of expertise?" If the cost of more managers seems high, I'd counter that having too few managers has contributed to ever escalating costs and stagnant, unacceptable outcomes. It also fuels staff burnout, turnover, and teacher shortages.

And don't forget that small and midsized districts can have teacher leaders fill many of these key roles for thousands of dollars in stipends, not tens of thousands in salary. Moreover, the business office, program evaluation, and teaching and learning leaders already exist and should be ready to step in to play their part as well.

Who reports to whom and where the lines on the org chart are drawn might seem like an academic exercise, but it's a key step in effectively implementing the six shifts. Updating special education and interventions for struggling students to meet twenty-first-century needs is no easy task. As the prior chapters detail, a lot has changed in the world since Gerald Ford signed the first special education law, and much must change in our schools to adapt to higher standards, needier students, and fewer resources. Upsizing, strengthening, and rethinking the management team is the glue that will hold all these other pieces together.

CHAPTER 9

Uniting Parents, Educators, and Policy Makers to Shift Special Education into the New Era

Congratulations, you have completed eight chapters that detail how to shift practices and services to better serve today's struggling students, with and without special needs. I hope just one question remains unanswered: Why haven't more districts already embraced these best practices and implemented the six shifts? They are better for kids, staff, and taxpayers. They are common sense, but still far from commonplace.

While no one seems happy with the status quo, moving away from the current, less than successful, less than cost-effective, less than stress-free practices has been difficult. I think we have had to settle for a system no one loves because change has been attempted piecemeal, and key stakeholders haven't had a seat at the table.

STONES, NOT ROSE PETALS

Improving special education and general education intervention has been risky business in the past. I remember when, years ago, the Massachusetts legislature took up a bill to increase access to general education supports for students with special needs. In a state long committed to inclusion and with a yawning achievement gap, this seemed like a good step in the right direction. It was in line with best practices and spurred in part by studies that showed students with disabilities received much less instruction from general educators, which in turn led to much lower achievement.

So, what happened when the legislature passed this smart reform? We will never know. It died a gruesome death. At the first public hearing, parents, students, and special educators swarmed the committee room. Kids in wheelchairs, on ventilators, and with severe disabilities packed the room. Parents cried, and at times screamed, that the well-intentioned changes would harm students. A few noted that some kids might die as a result. Only a few superintendents spoke in favor. No significant reform legislation has surfaced in the following twenty years.

On a smaller scale, one large district sought to move away from co-teaching and provide 100 percent core instruction, plus daily extra time, both from highly skilled content-strong staff. Clearly, this was a step in the right direction. The school board members didn't toss rose petals at the superintendent; they threw stones. Vicious attacks on the superintendent's concern for children's well-being led to a series of highly critical newspaper and TV stories, talk of a vote of no confidence, and a hasty retreat. Co-teaching and a huge achievement gap remained in place years later.

One lesson many folks draw from these and countless similar experiences is, don't mess with special education. That's how the achievement gap has persevered, staff burnout accelerates, and spending swells.

PUT KIDS AND STAFF NEEDS FIRST

My sense of why good people fight to hold on to past practice is they don't trust the motivation of those leading the reform effort. "You just want to save money" and "You are balancing the budget on the backs of the neediest students" are common shouts at public meetings. Even when the focus is on achievement, too often the impetus for change is the state flagging a school or district for low "subgroup scores." Few things are less motivating than change driven by the desire to please state accountability requirements.

If schools around the country are going to widely adopt the six shifts, their motivation must be righteous indignation, not financial gains or political cover. Shouldn't everyone want to help kids and teachers? Don't we owe all children the skills and knowledge to succeed after graduation? Don't teachers deserve a job that's sustainable for decades, that doesn't cut into their weekends, and that brings satisfaction from helping kids? The reform effort must be grounded in a sincere and heartfelt desire to help kids and staff.

Most of the reform-minded leaders I have met, including those who got hit with stones, figuratively, did have the right motivation, but they did a lousy job of convincing others. I count myself in this group. I need to make a confession. As a superintendent, I pushed through all six shifts in practice for struggling students, and the kids benefited greatly. That said, I created much outrage and too many hurt feelings. Politically I paid a steep price. Perhaps worst of all, many colleagues concluded that the dramatic increase in reading, math, and English scores, the tenfold expansion of mental health counseling, and the vastly improved behavioral supports we achieved just weren't worth the political cost. I did the right thing, the wrong way.

I pointed to flagging test scores and growing spending as proof that change was needed. I spent too much time pointing out that we had paraprofessionals and special educators who weren't content-strong teachers working with our neediest students. I harped on the data, and to some, it felt like I was blaming the staff. No wonder opposition arose as quickly as did support. I didn't need to be hit by too many stones before pausing and reconsidering my approach to reform. Over the years, I have learned that broad-based support is possible when people:

- *Focus on children's future.* The biggest shortcoming of special education and intervention services today is that too many kids won't be on track for a fulfilling, rewarding, financially stable life. As the job market demands higher skills for most middle-class jobs, we must prepare our students to step over this higher bar.

- *Remember that special educators are great folks doing what district leaders ask them to do.* Special educators didn't create the current system. They didn't ask to be assigned a hundred different tasks, many outside their field of expertise. They didn't create fifteen to twenty hours of paperwork and meetings each week. They just work hard trying to do all that we ask of them.

- *Recognize that helping teachers is as important as helping kids.* Too often, reform is positioned as moving from adult-centric decisions to student-centered ones. This is a false dichotomy. There will be no improvement for kids without also improving the life of the staff. Addressing the burnout of general educators and special educators alike is as important as closing the achievement gap.

- *Have empathy for past decisions.* It's easy to look at the status quo and wonder how we got here; we got here one logical step at a time. It started with wanting to serve a few children with severe disabilities. When special education expanded to meet the needs of a wider range of students, it mirrored many of the then current practices, especially substantially separate classrooms. Inclusion was a logical reaction to the overuse of separate classrooms, and paraprofessionals and co-teaching seemed a reasonable support for general education teachers who hadn't been trained in teaching students with disabilities. Finally, and sadly, some districts balked at meeting the requirements of the law, so lots of protections were provided, which unfortunately led to lots of meetings and paperwork. Every step was reasonable, but now the world has changed, and so must how we support students who struggle.

- *Are honest.* Being a district leader is as much about managing politics as it is about managing teaching and learning. Parents and teachers know the system isn't working for many students, but district leaders find it hard to say this publicly. A straightforward "Everyone cares, everyone is working hard, but we owe our children better" sets the right tone.

- *Address racial and economic inequities directly.* In many districts, children of color or those living in poverty are negatively impacted disproportionately by many of the shortcomings of current special education, intervention, and discipline practices. Share the data and own the data. The conversation is uncomfortable if you are more privileged, but you gain the credibility critical to building a coalition for change.
- *Give parents a seat at the table.* I don't have a child with a disability, so I would be disingenuous saying I know what parents must be feeling. But after hundreds, maybe even thousands of conversations, I know many are worried. They worry that their children are frustrated, won't have friends, aren't welcomed, or won't be successful after graduation. They worry a lot that change could make these situations worse, not better. Their concerns are reasonable. For thirty years, districts have struggled to improve academic, social, emotional, behavioral, and life outcomes for children like theirs.

PARENTS AS PARTNERS

Sweeping change isn't possible without active parent support. This support will need to be earned through dialogue and welcoming them into the reform effort. The one and only smart process decision I made as superintendent was reaching out to the parents of students with special needs and inviting them to be partners for progress. They, better than anyone else, understood the need for change, and they vocally championed the shift to best practices.

Given years of distrust and failed promises for improvement, their support didn't come quickly. I met with representatives for a few hours every month for three years. I needed to invest in them if they were going to invest in the reform effort. Most importantly, I listened more than I spoke. This was a forum to learn about their concerns and to test-drive new plans. It also highlighted potential potholes I might have missed. They in turn shared with a much wider group the benefits and safeguards of our improvement efforts.

No reform effort can take hold without strong parent support, but sometimes they do lead the opposition. Sometimes parents advocate for the status quo. This is most visible when it comes to the bold, good-for-kids shift toward content-strong staff. Unintentionally, many parents fight this needed change.

Why do some parents fight having their kids taught by teachers who are experts in their subject, with a track record of raising achievement? Because they are focusing on the loss, not the gain. Part of this shift to content-strong teachers is a change in IEP language and less time with paraprofessionals. Reducing paraprofessional services makes way for increasing content-strong teacher support. Kids don't have enough time in the day for both, and districts must shift the budget from non-certified folks to fund additional certified staff.

One superintendent learned the hard way just how much push-back she could generate by doing the right thing. Alarmed at the ever-growing reliance on paraprofessionals supporting elementary students who struggled to read, she announced a modest reduction in para-professional staffing levels (from really high to still very high). Unfortunately, she made the statement during a budget presentation and opened with a litany of the shortcomings of the current situation. Parents of students with special needs balked, loudly. Some feared the cuts were definite, and the reading teachers just a hope. Others were concerned that all paraprofessionals would be let go, and thus critical supports would vanish. Kids with health or behavior needs, for example, didn't need reading teachers; they needed paraprofessionals. The parents came to multiple school board meetings to voice strong opposition, until the board overruled the superintendent. The parents clapped, and the board members smiled. They had guaranteed that students who couldn't read well would continue to receive instruction from noncertified staff, some of whom didn't read well themselves. Vilifying a superintendent trying to do the right thing helps no one. (See the sidebar "A Special Note to Parents and Advocates: Don't Hate Superintendents for Doing Their Job" for a new way to interact with district leaders.)

A SPECIAL NOTE TO PARENTS AND ADVOCATES: DON'T HATE SUPERINTENDENTS FOR DOING THEIR JOB

Saving money is not a good reason to change special education. Improving outcomes for students and improving work life for teachers is. But saving money isn't a bad thing, while the district raises achievement and makes teaching less stressful.

While no district can improve supports for students who struggle without active parent support, the superintendent also needs to be a strong leader. The first job of a district leader is to serve students and teachers well. Close behind, however, is doing the most good for the most students with the limited funds available. Fortunately, the results of the six shifts are great for kids and adults, and the efforts cost the same or less than current ones in most districts.

Historically, most efforts to better serve students who struggle focused on more adults. More adults means more spending, and seldom did towns, states, or the federal government provide all these extra funds. Today, despite the lack of progress, parents and advocates commonly still demand more adults, thus more spending. This dynamic makes some district leaders gun-shy of starting a candid conversation about improving supports for students who struggle, with and without disabilities.

A very caring committed superintendent announced a multiyear commitment to implement all six shifts in practice. Rather than shouts of thanks or murmurs of gratitude, the first angry question was, "Are you trying to save money?" The superintendent responded, "Yes. As we implement more effective core instruction and better interventions, fewer students might need special ed services. As we streamline meetings and paperwork, staffing will drift down over time." Parents erupted in anger, and quietly the district backed away from making any shifts. Low results and calm remained.

Thankfully, the superintendent didn't accept unacceptable outcomes. The next year she approached the situation very differently, by:

1. Documenting how many kids received reading help from paraprofessionals.
2. Focusing on the gain, a commitment to highly skilled reading teachers.

3. Making this a moral issue, not a budgetary one. The plan was presented by the chief academic officer, months before the budget season began.
4. Being clear that these changes didn't impact students who needed paraprofessional support for behavior, autism, safety or severe needs.

This time there was broad parental support.

Parents need to be partners, and building trust is key to a winning partnership. I remember a very tense meeting with sixty or so parents of students with special needs. They were angry with the district. They had every reason to be. Despite good intentions, district staff missed state-mandated deadlines for IEP meetings. Despite active recruitment, vacancies in staffing led to promised services not being provided. Perhaps most infuriating of all, past leadership had tried to minimize the problems, denied them when it could, and focused on the causes, not the solutions.

I wanted to be different. I acknowledged our shortcomings, shared our plans to right the wrong, and empathized with the parents' anger. This diffused the situation for the moment. I promised to meet again in thirty days to update them on progress. After three or four of these monthly updates, the tension in the room diminished.

Unfortunately, not being angry isn't the same as building trust. At our next meeting, which had become a regular, monthly, unscripted session, I shared our plans to increase the number of reading teachers, funded by a decrease in paraprofessionals. Rather than giving thanks, they erupted. Before I had finished the overview, mothers were texting their advocates and drafting emails to storm the next school board meeting; tension filled the room again. Surprised and disappointed, I tried a new tact, straight talk.

I decided to drop the polite, safe, public pronouncement style of communication that superintendents typically rely on. Straight talk included sharing good news and bad. The district shared monthly reports on meeting timelines, staffing vacancies, and missed services. We created a hot line for suggestions or frustrations. As importantly, district leaders shared, in classroom style, best practices for helping struggling students. We discussed articles and had guest speakers. Perhaps the riskiest step, we shared the national statistics on how unacceptable the life outcomes for too many students with disabilities were. In short, we opened up to the fact that the system wasn't serving their children well. We made the point that meeting timelines and providing services on time was required, but insufficient. Only then did the parents start to support the shift toward reading, math, and English teachers.

Some still flinched at reducing paraprofessional support. All my statistics and research couldn't sway them. Only when I asked parents of former students with special needs to speak with the group, did we win over the majority. A mother of a twenty-five-year-old teared up as she shared that she had fought to "get a para," fought even harder "to keep the para," and rejoiced when her son graduated and was hugged by his paraprofessional as he crossed the stage. She summarized, "You see, we lost every time we thought we won. The day after graduation, the para was gone, and my son lacked the independence, self-advocacy, and problem-solving skills to succeed after graduation. Mistakenly, we focused on getting through school, not getting through life."

The broader point of the story is that lots of honest conversation, sharing, and dialogue created trust. Trust created a wave of support from parents that encouraged the school board to make sweeping shifts in how to meet the needs of all struggling students, including those with disabilities.

ATTRITION IS YOUR FRIEND

One reason, maybe the most common reason, for lack of support in implementing the six shifts isn't because folks think they won't help kids, but rather that they might hurt some adults. Shift #3, content-strong expertise, sounds great, until the moment staffing plans are built. Often, as districts begin this shift, they realize they are short on reading teachers, math teachers, behaviorists, and mental health counselors. As these skilled teachers are added, they reduce the caseload of parapro-fessionals and others.

The worst thing a district can do is try to implement the six shifts without staff who have the requisite expertise. The second worse thing it can do is to pull the rug out from under dedicated staff, who, through no fault of their own, lack some of the needed skills. The best path forward is to phase in the staffing changes at the rate of attrition. As vacancies arise, ask the question, "What is the skill, experience, and expertise we need most?" Often this might mean filling a few parapro-fessional openings with a certified reading teacher, back-filling a gener-alist special educator with one specifically screened and hired to focus on behavior or IEP management, for example. Some districts are filling hard-to-fill special education vacancies with general education math or English teachers who will provide interventions historically provided by special educators. Announcing at the start of a commitment to the six shifts that no one will lose their job as a result of the shift to con-tent expertise and playing to strengths help build a broader coalition for change.

PUBLIC POLICY: THE HELPING HAND OF GOVERNMENT?

Shifting practice to best meet the needs of struggling students is hard work. State and federal policy can make it easier or nearly impossi-ble. Without the groundbreaking efforts of policy makers in the 1970s, there would be no guaranteed supports for students with disabilities. Without the bipartisan commitment to accountability, we wouldn't have the proof that more and better is needed. As the world shifts, so must policy.

The irony of the current policy debate is that policy makers seem to fully support all six shifts, while the policies themselves are stubbornly preventing their implementation. (For more on unintended conse-quences of policy, see the sidebar "Hurting While Trying to Help: The Unintended Consequences of Current Policy.") I remember walking into the belly of the beast at 400 Maryland Ave. in Washington, DC.

HURTING WHILE TRYING TO HELP: THE UNINTENDED CONSEQUENCES OF CURRENT POLICY

Special education regulations are set at the federal level and often have extra requirements that differ state by state. Some very common regulations or interpretation of regulations are in direct odds with best practices, including:

- **Valuing certification over expertise.** Go figure. It is legal for a certified special educator with no training skill or aptitude to teach a special ed math class or provide special education intervention, but a cracker-jack certified math teacher can't.
- **Reimbursing special educators but not reading specialists, math teachers, or other general educators.** In the states that don't formally discourage general education intervention, many discourage it financially. If a special educator provides the service, some states reimburse some or a lot of the cost, but if an experienced, certified reading teacher, for example, did the same thing, the district wouldn't get a cent of reimbursement.
- **Turning a blind eye to noncertified teachers hiding in plain sight.** No Child Left Behind was supposed to ensure that only highly qualified teachers provide instruction to students. Special education students are regularly taught by paraprofessionals who aren't teachers, and it's okay in every state.
- **Providing guarantees for some struggling students, but not all.** If a student struggles to read, for example, and they have a disability, the law is swift and powerful to ensure extra help. If a classmate struggles just as much, but doesn't have a disability, it's up to the goodwill of districts to rectify the situation.
- **Prioritizing spending more than high-quality services.** A unique aspect of special education is the requirement of districts to maintain spending from the prior year, the so-called maintenance-of-effort requirement. Intended to ensure that tight budgets aren't balanced at the expense of the neediest students, this well-intentioned regulation equates spending with helping. For example, say an untrained paraprofessional works with one student for thirty minutes each day. Alternatively, a certified reading teacher works with five students, each struggling with phonics for forty-five minutes a day. Because the second option costs less, such a shift, if done districtwide, could run afoul of maintenance-of-effort requirements. More service, of higher quality, is counted as less.

(continues)

- **Getting angrier over missed timelines than limited learning.** Yes, compliance is important, but learning should matter most. Typically, chronic noncompliance with timelines brings forceful corrective action, monitoring, and unrelenting pressure. Chronic achievement gaps are taken seriously, but the reaction and support are more muted.

A coalition of stakeholders is needed that will lead the way in creating policies and regulations that ease implementing the six shifts. Kids deserve nothing less.

I had snagged a listening lunch with Arne Duncan, then secretary of education. The setup was simple, like a silent shark tank. Four guests each had fifteen minutes to share one idea with Arne. This was the first airing of the six shifts.

He listened but didn't let on what he thought. Since the ideas mostly repudiated current policy, I assumed he wouldn't receive them well. A few weeks later, I was invited back to share the ideas in more detail with his entire cabinet. That was a pleasant surprise, but much more surprising was the next offer to return. Would I share, in even more detail, the six shifts with the assistant secretary for special education and rehabilitative services and his leadership team. Now I was getting nervous. How could I tell the folks who built, run, and maintain special education as we know it that it was no longer aligned with the times?

After ten minutes of polite euphemisms hinting at the need for change, I realized I was boring them. So, in desperation, I started telling them what I really thought. Sandwiched between a few "no disrespect intended," I laid out what kids with mild to moderate disabilities really needed and how current policy and practice hurt as much as helped. Their response: "We know, we agree, and we are trying to fix it!" I was shocked.

I have had similar conversations with leaders in departments of education in Massachusetts, California, New Mexico, Pennsylvania, Vermont, Ohio, and elsewhere. It turns out, lots of people want to update special education, but building a coalition to support the changes remains elusive. I have long wondered if all the key stakeholders got in one room, might they realize that they all want the same thing and realize that mistrust, not divergent views, maintains the status quo.

VERMONT LEADS THE WAY

In Vermont, disappointing outcomes and escalating costs brought special education to the forefront in the state. The secretary of education, the superintendents, special education directors, school boards, and principals all saw the need for change. Parents and teachers wanted better, too. Over the course of a few years, the state and the various associations (superintendents, special education directors, etc.) met in the same room and partnered with my firm to rethink special education and support for struggling students across the state. After lots of presentations, studies, proof points by forward-thinking districts, and conversations, it seemed almost everyone wanted to embrace the six shifts. One obstacle remained. State law supported, encouraged, reinforced, and even rewarded the old behavior and greatly hindered the new.

When the conversation turned to changing legislation, not surprisingly the Vermont house and senate weren't eager to grab onto this third-rail issue. At the initial hearing, they were surprised to learn that nearly every stakeholder group wanted change and wanted the same changes. With the help of some smart people from the University of Vermont and the tireless support of the association leaders and the agency of education, a clear plan was developed. A sweeping reform bill, Act 173, passed the house unanimously and, a few months later, passed the senate and was signed into law. Among the most important changes, the law:

- Blurred the line between general education and special education by proclaiming that all struggling students should be helped, in similar ways, whether they had a disability or not.
- Prioritized core instruction and extra time to learn and placed the highest value on the strongest teachers providing extra help.

- Elevated the role of social, emotional, and behavioral supports.
- Paved the way for funding general educators to have a much larger role in supporting struggling students, including those with IEPs.

The work in Vermont is far from done, and slews of rules need to be rewritten to turn broad policy into real changes on the ground, but it shows the power of a broad-based coalition.

SEVEN STEPS TO BUILDING THE COALITION OF THE BOLD

I hope that the first chapter stirred you to want to take action and the next seven revealed what actions to take. To close, let's map out the seven guidelines that might build the coalition of the bold who will change the trajectory of the lives of students who struggle, with and without disabilities.

1. Declare, without blame, that the status quo isn't good enough.
2. Acknowledge that the world has changed, and so must special education and intervention.
3. Build trust with parents through honest two-way dialogue.
4. Make the future better for teachers, not just students.
5. Embrace teamwork between special educators and general education.
6. Worry more about outcomes than timelines or spending.
7. Don't forget that social, emotional, and behavioral supports matter just as much as academics.

Good luck. You can do it. The kids are counting on you.

The future for students who struggle can be bright. This story can have a happy ending for students, teachers, and even taxpayers. The road to this conclusion is only possible if a coalition of the bold makes it so. Parents, teachers (general education and special education alike), special education leaders, principals, superintendents, school boards, and legislators need to join hands and demand that supports for struggling students shift to meet the needs of a new era.

NOTES

CHAPTER 1

1. Sarah D. Sparks, "Low Scorers Losing Ground on NAEP," *Education Week*, April 25, 2018, https://www.edweek.org/ew/articles/2018/04/25/low-scorers -losing-ground-on-naep.html.
2. National Center for Education Statistics, National Assessment of Educational Progress (NAEP), 2017 Reading Assessment, Average Scale Scores and Percentages at Each Achievement Level for Grade 8 Reading, by All Students [TOTAL] and Jurisdiction, via NAEP Data Explorer, https://www.nationsreportcard.gov /ndecore/xplore/nde.
3. US Department of Education, Institute of Education Sciences, National Center for Education Statistics, National Assessment of Educational Progress (NAEP), 2017 Reading Assessment, Percentages at Each Achievement Level for Grade 4 Reading, by Disability Status of Student, Excluding Those with 504 Plan [IEP2009] and Jurisdiction via NAEP Data Explorer, https://www.nations reportcard.gov/ndecore/xplore/nde
4. National Center for Educational Achievement (NCEA), "Catching Up to College and Career Readiness," ACT, Inc., 2012, https://www.act.org/content/dam /act/unsecured/documents/Catching-Up-To-College-and-Career-Readiness.pdf.
5. US Department of Education, Laws & Guidance, Elementary & Secondary Education, Special Education—Technical Assistance on State Data Collection—IDEA General Supervision Enhancement Grant, IDEA Section 618 Data Products: State Level Data Files, Part B, Personnel, 2005-2017, data reported by states to the US Department of Education's Office of Special Education Programs (OSEP) for the first time on May 1, 2011, https://www2.ed.gov/programs/osepidea/618 -data/state-level-data-files/index.html; US Department of Education, National Center for Education Statistics, 2019, Digest of Education Statistics, 2017 (NCES 2018-070), chapter 2, https://nces.ed.gov/fastfacts/display.asp?id=64 and https://fordhaminstitute.org/national/research/shifting-trends-special-education.
6. Multiple Sources compiled and cited in "About the Shortage," National Coalition on Personnel Shortages in Special Education and Related Services, https:// specialedshortages.org/about-the-shortage/.

CHAPTER 2

1. John Hattie, *Visible Learning: A Synthesis of Over 800 Meta-Analyses Relating to Achievement* (London: Routledge, 2013); Linda Darling-Hammond, "Teacher Quality and Student Achievement," *Education Policy Analysis Archives* 8 (2000): 1; Jennifer King Rice, "Teacher Quality: Understanding the Effectiveness of Teacher Attributes," *Economic Policy Institute*, Washington, DC, 2003; "Teachers Matter: Understanding Teachers' Impact on Student Achievement" (Santa Monica, CA: RAND Corporation, 2012), https://www.rand.org/pubs/corporate_pubs/CP693z1-2012-09.html; Laura Goe and Leslie M. Stickler, "Teacher Quality and Student Achievement: Making the Most of Recent Research. TQ Research & Policy Brief," National Comprehensive Center for Teacher Quality, 2008; Douglas N. Harris and Tim R. Sass, "Teacher Training, Teacher Quality and Student Achievement," *Journal of Public Economics* 95, no. 7 (2011): 798–812.

2. US Department of Education, Institute of Education Sciences, National Center for Education Statistics, National Assessment of Educational Progress (NAEP), 2011 Reading Assessment.

3. Stephen Sawchuk, "Unlocking STEM Pathways for All Students," *Education Week*, May 23, 2018, https://www.edweek.org/ew/articles/2018/05/23/unlocking-stem-pathways-for-all-students.html.

4. Thomas Hehir, Todd Grindal, and Hadas Eidelman, "Review of Special Education in the Commonwealth of Massachusetts" (Boston: Massachusetts Department of Elementary and Secondary Education, 2012), http://www.doe.mass.edu/sped/hehir/2012-04sped.pdf.

5. US Department of Education, Laws & Guidance, Elementary & Secondary Education, Special Education—Technical Assistance on State Data Collection—IDEA General Supervision Enhancement Grant, IDEA Section 618 Data Products: State Level Data Files, Part B, Personnel, 2005–2017, data reported by states to the US Department of Education's Office of Special Education Programs (OSEP) for the first time on May 1, 2011 https://www2.ed.gov/programs/osepidea/618-data/state-level-data-files/index.html; US Department of Education, National Center for Education Statistics, 2019, Digest of Education Statistics, 2017 (NCES 2018-070), Chapter 2, https://nces.ed.gov/fastfacts/display.asp?id=64.

CHAPTER 3

1. US Department of Education, Institute of Education Sciences, National Center for Education Statistics, National Assessment of Educational Progress (NAEP), 2017 Reading Assessment, Average Scale Scores and Percentages at Each Achievement Level for Grade 4 Reading, by All Students [TOTAL] and Jurisdiction: 2017, https://www.nationsreportcard.gov/ndecore/xplore/nde.

2. National Council on Teacher Quality, "Strengthening Reading Instruction through Better Preparation of Elementary and Special Education Teachers,"

August 2018, https://www.nctq.org/dmsView/Strengthening_Reading _Instruction_Databurst.

3. John Hattie, "Hattie Effect Size List—256 Influences Related to Achievement," Visible Learning, December 2017, https://visible-learning.org/hattie-ranking -influences-effect-sizes-learning-achievement/.

4. Jade Wexler et al., "Reading Comprehension and Co-Teaching Practices in Middle School English Language Arts Classrooms," *Exceptional Children* 84, no. 4 (July 2018): 384–402.

CHAPTER 4

1. US Department of Education, Laws & Guidance, Elementary & Secondary Education, Special Education—Technical Assistance on State Data Collection— IDEA General Supervision Enhancement Grant, IDEA Section 618 Data Products: State Level Data Files, Part B, Personnel, 2005–2017, data reported by states to the US Department of Education's Office of Special Education Programs (OSEP) available at https://www2.ed.gov/programs/osepidea/618-data /state-level-data-files/index.html; US Department of Education, National Center for Education Statistics, Statistics of Public Elementary and Secondary School Systems, 1980-81; Common Core of Data (CCD), "State Nonfiscal Survey of Public Elementary/Secondary Education," 1985-86 through 2015-16; and National Elementary and Secondary Enrollment Projection Model, 1972 through 2027 available at https://nces.ed.gov/programs/digest /d17/tables/dt17_203.10.asp.

2. Gary T. Henry and Kevin C. Bastian, "Measuring Up: The National Council on Teacher Quality's Ratings of Teacher Preparation Programs and Measures of Teacher Performance," University of North Carolina, 2015, https://public policy.unc.edu/files/2017/03/NCTQ-Revised.pdf.

3. National Council on Teacher Quality, "Strengthening Reading Instruction through Better Preparation of Elementary and Special Education Teachers," August 2018, https://www.nctq.org/dmsView/Strengthening_Reading _Instruction_Databurst.

4. David Blazar, Blake Heller, and Thomas J Kane et al., *Learning by the Book: Comparing math achievement growth by textbook in six Common Core states*, Research Report (Cambridge, MA: Center for Education Policy Research, Harvard University, 2019).

5. Bruce Joyce and Beverly Showers, *Student Achievement Through Staff Development*, 3rd ed. (Alexandria, VA: Association for Supervision & Curriculum Development, 2002).

6. US Department of Education, Institute of Education Sciences, National Center for Education Statistics, National Assessment of Educational Progress (NAEP), 2017 Reading Assessment, Average Scale Scores and Percentages at Each Achievement Level for Grade 8 Reading, by All Students [TOTAL] and

Jurisdiction, via NAEP Data Explorer, available at https://www.nationsreport-card.gov/ndecore/xplore/nde.

CHAPTER 5

1. Evie Blad, "Schools Grapple with Student Depression as Data Show Problem Worsening," *Education Week*, March 20, 2019, https://www.edweek.org/ew/articles/2019/03/14/schools-grapple-with-student-depression-as-data.html.

2. Eleanor Craft and Aimee Howley, "African-American Students' Experience in Special Education Programs," *Teachers College Record* 120, no. 10 (October 2018): 1–35.

3. For more on alternative schools, see *District Management Journal*, Fall 2017.

4. US Government Accountability Office, "K–12 Education: Discipline Disparities for Black Students, Boys, and Students with Disabilities," Report to Congressional Requestors, March 2018, GAO-18-258, 14, https://www.gao.gov/assets/700/690828.pdf.

5. Sarah D. Sparks, "Suspension Rates Higher for Students of Color with Disabilities," *Education Week*, April 24, 2018, https://blogs.edweek.org/edweek/inside-school-research/2018/04/Civil_Rights_data_discipline_gaps_special_education.html.

6. US Department of Education Office for Civil Rights, Civil Rights Data Collection, Data Snapshot: School Discipline, Issue Brief No. 1, March 21, 2014, citing 2011-12 data, https://www2.ed.gov/about/offices/list/ocr/docs/crdc-discipline-snapshot.pdf.

7. Jim Dillon, "Are we jumping to SEL?" *Smartbrief*, June 20, 2018, https://www.smartbrief.com/original/2018/06/are-we-jumping-sel

8. Denisa R. Superville, "Student Centered Schools," *Education Week*, March 13, 2019, https://www.edweek.org/ew/articles/2019/03/13/these-students-are-doing-pd-with-their.html.

9. Matt Krentz et al. "Fixing the Flawed Approach to Diversity," Boston Consulting Group, January 27, 2019, https://www.bcg.com/en-us/publications/2019/fixing-the-flawed-approach-to-diversity.aspx.

CHAPTER 7

1. Emily Hanford, "Why Millions of Kids Can't Read and What Better Teaching Can Do About It," NPR, January 2, 2019, https://www.npr.org/2019/01/02/677722959/why-millions-of-kids-cant-read-and-what-better-teaching-can-do-about-it.

2. "Optimal Scheduling for Secondary School Students," Hanover Research, 2014, https://www.gssaweb.org/optimal-scheduling-for-secondary-school-students-2/.

ABOUT THE AUTHOR

NATHAN LEVENSON is the managing director of the District Management Group in Boston. Levenson began his career in the private sector, starting as a strategic planning management consultant, owner of a midsized manufacturer of highly engineered machinery, and a turnaround consultant helping struggling firms. A passion for public education led to a career switch that included six years as a school board member; assistant superintendent for curriculum and instruction in Harvard, Massachusetts; and superintendent of the Arlington, Massachusetts, public schools.

Levenson was hired as a change agent in Arlington during a turbulent time in a divided community. He oversaw all academic and operational aspects of a district with nine schools and a budget of over $50 million. Levenson's leadership led to wide-scale changes in academic programs by accelerating the move to standards-based education and teacher-developed common formative assessments in reading, math, writing, and social studies.

He helped create and champion an intensive reading program that reduced the number of students reading below grade level by two-thirds and revamped special education services, leading to a 24 percent improvement in academic achievement in English and math. The Rennie Center for Education Research and Policy identified Arlington High as a best-practice school for reducing the special education achievement gap by more than that of nearly all other public schools in the state (a 66 percent reduction in the achievement gap). Much of this effort focused on cost effectively improving MTSS and special education services.

As a strong believer in the importance of developing staff, Levenson implemented a new system for hiring teachers and brought an emphasis on creating teamwork between administrators and teams of teachers, despite an environment that had prized isolation and turf conflict. Collaboration was based on the work of Richard DuFour's professional learning community and Patrick Lencioni's book *The Five Dysfunctions of a Team.* Levenson created a less hierarchal climate within schools and departments, resulting in the creation of fifty teacher leadership roles and true distributed leadership.

Putting the phrase "It takes a village to raise a child" into action, the Arlington Public Schools built partnerships with local nonprofits to provide—at little or no cost—psychiatric counselors, social workers, family counseling, a diversion program, drug and alcohol counseling, and a communitywide coalition to help keep students safe from substance abuse and stress.

As managing director of the District Management Group, Levenson assists school districts across the country in raising achievement during times of declining resources. His work in special education is on the leading edge of thinking and practice, and his support of districts with strategic planning, resource allocation, cost-effective teaching and learning strategies, and human capital development is also at the forefront of the nation's school reform efforts.

He has overseen a number of national and statewide studies on special education including an analysis of special education costs and outcomes from fourteen hundred districts nationally and a study of best practices and related staffing for struggling students in all districts in Massachusetts. One such study was profiled in a *Wall Street Journal* editorial and led to a private discussion of his work with education secretary Arne Duncan and a number of follow-up discussions with his senior team. Levenson has been an adviser to state departments of education, has contributed to think tanks, and is a regular speaker on the topic of improving special education and services for struggling students.

His work has been profiled in the *District Management Journal* and in The Rennie Center for Education Research and Policy's best practices in special education report, and chronicled in *Stretching the School Dollar*, published by the Harvard Education Press. He has published research for the American Enterprise Institute, Center for American Progress, The Fordham Foundation, and the Bill and Melinda Gates Foundation.

Levenson received a BA from Dartmouth College and an MBA with distinction from Harvard Business School, and is a graduate of the Broad Foundation Superintendents Academy.

INDEX